ISBN: 978-0-578-33879-8 (hardcover)

WHEN YOUR NAME IS ON THE DOOR

An Inside Look at How Harvey Massey
Built an American Service Industry Giant

BRUCE F. "BUD" KATZ

TABLE OF CONTENTS

PFC Harvey L. Massey, US Army Security Agency, circa 1961

Chapter 1

Before Massey Services

"Life is what happens to us while we're making other plans."

Paraphrasing from the book of Proverbs 19:21, the author Michael Chabon once wrote, "Man makes plans...and God laughs."

In 1963, Harvey Massey was not yet twenty-two years of age. But he had a plan.

The young man, who was born on December 28, 1941, and grew up in Melville, Louisiana, had just been honorably discharged from the United States Army at Ft. Devens in Massachusetts. Melville, which sits on the banks of the Atchafalaya River in St. Landry Parish, today has a population of just over a thousand people. When Harvey Massey was growing up, the town had nearly twice that. Melville is a few minutes shy of an hour west from Baton Rouge and just over two hours from New Orleans in the same direction.

In 1959, he graduated from Melville High School, where he was a solid student and standout basketball player. He dated a local girl for a while, had a band called Harvey & The Saints, and worked in his grandfather's general store and his father's penny-a-pound ice business before enlisting in the US Army and being assigned to the Army Security Agency.

People who work in the security apparatus of the American armed forces typically don't talk much about the specifics of what they did, even more than a half century after they did it. Harvey

Harvey Massey at Twelve Years of Age

is no exception. But he does talk about his Roman Catholic faith. He does talk about having served his country. And he does talk about a pretty, young blonde girl, Carol Nisula, who he met while attending a church social function about twenty minutes west of Ft. Devens in the Leominster-Fitchburg area of Worcester County, Massachusetts.

Now, most young men of twenty-two might have been expected to return home upon receiving an honorable discharge from the US Army to spend time with family, renew friendships, and certainly begin considering next steps. But not this young man.

You see, this young man, Harvey Massey, had a plan.

While Harvey was serving his country, Carol Nisula had moved to Austin, Texas, where her

Carol Nisula, approximately seventeen years old

father worked in tool and die manufacturing. Later, and with an honorable discharge in hand, Harvey made a quick stop in Melville to visit with his mother, Margaret, and his older sister, Mary Ellen, before heading off to the hometown of the Texas Longhorns and capital of the Lone Star State. He was single-minded in his purpose to make sure it was he who got to spend the rest of his life alongside that particular pretty young blonde.

The other part of Harvey's plan included establishing himself in a growing community, which Austin was, and getting involved in the real estate business, something in which he'd always been interested. While he was in the Army, Harvey made the acquaintance of several officers who spoke glowingly about giving real estate a try after they left the service.

"You know, Harvey, there's only so much land. God's not making any more of it."

"You know, Harvey, the one thing every man in America aspires to is to own his own home."

"You know, Harvey, every real estate transaction is potentially two transactions. There's always a buyer, and there's always a seller. That means there's possibly two commissions on every sale!"

Harvey was an enlisted man. These were officers. Enlisted men paid attention to officers.

Soon after he arrived in Austin, Harvey Massey made an appointment with the most successful and well-known real estate broker in town. The broker had two questions for Harvey: "What do you know about Austin?" and "How many people do you know in Austin?"

Harvey was, and still is, nothing if not scrupulously honest. He replied, "Not much and not many."

The broker encouraged him to get a job—any job—so he

could get to know Austin and get to know as many people as possible.

Three days later, on February 1, 1963, Harvey Massey began working with Orkin Exterminating Company. The company, which would be purchased by Rollins, Inc. out of Atlanta, Georgia, in 1964, was, at that time, on track to become the largest pest control operation in America and the world.

And so, the first leg of Harvey's remarkable, perhaps singular journey, from then to now, had officially begun.

• • •

For many years, members of his family, his senior staff, his friends, and industry colleagues have encouraged Harvey Massey to write a book. He's always offered the same response: "I'm not old enough to write a book."

As evidenced by this publication, apparently, now he is.

At the beginning of 2022, Massey Services finds itself in its thirty-seventh year of uninterrupted growth, much of it in the double digits. The company, which technically began in February 1985 as the highly leveraged, $3.9 million purchase of a stagnant, fifty-year-old, Orlando, Florida-based family business, is on track to generate over $318 million in revenue. The company has grown from 4 service centers to nearly 170 service centers by the end of 2021. There are, as this book goes to print, 2,300 vehicles in the Massey Services fleet and almost 2,500 team members, all providing outstanding service to over 750,000 customers in nine states.

"I've finally been convinced that future generations of our Massey family, including my and Carol's ten grandchildren, our leadership team members and their families, our industry colleagues, our community partners, and perhaps others, might benefit from knowing the story of how we've managed to build one of the most respected service operations in America," he said. "When you get to a certain age and to a certain place in life, you want to be the one to tell your own story."

When Your Name Is On the Door is Harvey Massey's own story, told mostly in his own words.

• • •

Soon after signing on with Orkin in early 1963 as a sales inspector, Harvey arrived at the first of many crossroads. He learned almost immediately that before he could sell Orkin's services, he needed to spend a little time learning about those services. He vividly recalls the moment. It was his first actual day of fieldwork. He was about seventy miles north of Austin, on his back, in a crawl space, under a house in Killeen, Texas, inspecting for evidence of termite infestation.

He distinctly recalls asking himself, "What the heck is a bright young man like me doing on his back, under a house, at 2:30 in the afternoon, in Killeen, Texas?"

The bright young man knew he needed to speed things up if he were to move forward to the point where he wouldn't have to do this sort of thing in August, when it gets really hot in Killeen, Texas.

Instead, on August 24, 1963, he and Carol said their I-dos at St. Ignatius Roman Catholic Church in Austin, Texas.

Harvey and Carol Massey, August 24, 1963, Austin, Texas

By early 1965, Harvey had become the top salesperson in South Texas. This was a good thing, because in March 1964, Harvey and Carol welcomed—two-plus months premature— the arrival of the first of their three children, three-pound, three-ounce Angela, into the world.

A career in the real estate business in Austin, Texas, was quickly entering Harvey's rearview mirror.

During the ensuing sixteen years, Harvey Massey's meteoric career with Orkin took him all over the nation. Austin led to San Antonio, then to Houston. Every move came with a pro- motion, including the one to district sales manager for Indiana, Illinois, and Ohio in 1968 that relocated him and his growing family to Indianapolis.

His journey up the Orkin ladder would take him, Carol, Angela, and their son, Tony, born in San Antonio in September 1966, to Waukegan and then LaSalle, Illinois. While in LaSalle, their third child, Andrea, was born in July 1972. Harvey's next move would deposit him and the family in Atlanta, Orkin's home base, as district manager for Georgia.

Angela, four, Tony, two, and Andrea, six months

This was a big move. It put Harvey Massey and his now complete nuclear family under the heat and light of Orkin's senior staff, including O. Wayne Rollins, CEO of Rollins, Inc., parent company of Orkin.

Although he was only in Atlanta for fifteen months, Harvey caught the eye of Earl Geiger, chief operating officer at Rollins, Inc., who became his mentor and close friend.

"I can't overstate the influence Earl Geiger had on my career in those years," Harvey said. "His friendship, wisdom, and generosity helped me more than I could ever have imagined. I will always feel blessed to have met him and to have been able to call him my friend."

Earl Geiger, far right, with other Rollins/Orkin executives

There will be more about Earl Geiger as *When Your Name Is On the Door* unfolds.

In 1974, eleven years into his ascent with Orkin, Harvey Massey was called into the office of Rollins, Inc. chairman O. Wayne Rollins. Harvey knew he wasn't there to chat about the Atlanta Braves. After some niceties, Mr. Rollins—as Harvey always referred to the big boss—invited the Massey family to hit the road once again. Harvey left that meeting promoted to the position of vice president. At thirty-two, he was the youngest vice president in Orkin's history. His job was to oversee the company's Midwest region while based in Chicago.

The family lived in Illinois for three years before opportunity again came knocking. If his promotion to vice president of Orkin's Midwest region was big, his next move would put him right into the middle of all the action at the world's largest pest control company. In January 1977, Harvey, Carol, and their three children returned to Atlanta as Harvey assumed the position of vice president for Orkin's central region.

Harvey Massey's rise within Orkin's hierarchy put him on track to someday be considered for the presidency of the company. His achievements in the field were unprecedented. He demonstrated virtually every leadership quality valued by O. Wayne Rollins, the man at the helm of the company. He also continued a wonderful and important relationship with Earl Geiger, the number two person at Rollins, Inc., Orkin's parent company.

But there was a problem. An obstacle. Actually, there were two obstacles: Randall Rollins and Gary Rollins, O. Wayne's two sons. Both were already jockeying for position as the next Rollins to lead Rollins, Inc., and the Orkin Exterminating Company.

Undeterred, Harvey Massey did what he always did. He excelled at growing revenues in Orkin's central region—its home region—and providing Orkin's customers with excellent service. He made sure the company's receivables were collected, that expenses were controlled, and he made certain to recruit and develop only the highest-quality people.

But, after two years of outstanding performance, he understood the limitations before him.

In March 1979, after sixteen years of skyrocketing up the ladder at the largest company in the pest control industry, Harvey cut the cord and accepted the position of senior vice president for operations at Terminix International, headquartered in Memphis, Tennessee. It was bittersweet, but he'd gone as far as was possible with Orkin.

Harvey understood the enormous challenge before him. Orkin was number one. Terminix was number two but far behind. The charge he was given was simple: close the gap.

Harvey Massey has always viewed himself, first and foremost, as a salesman. His earliest jobs back in Melville, Louisiana, involved taking care of customers in his grandfather's general store and selling and delivering for his father's ice business. He started out in the residential and commercial services industry inspecting homes and selling termite protection. He'd learned, early in his career, the importance business owners and operators place on growth. If a business isn't growing, it's shrinking. This tenet endures as one of his core beliefs about business.

As he'd moved up the ladder at Orkin, he learned the operational necessities of the service business. His title at Terminix may have been Senior Vice President for Operations, but he knew the people who hired him had done so because they believed, as he did, that the primary focus in business was growth.

During his time at Terminix, the company grew. And grew. And grew. From $40 million in annual revenue to over $100 million. Under Harvey Massey's leadership, the gap between number two and number one in the pest control industry had been substantially narrowed.

• • •

Near the end of 1984, Harvey learned that his friend and mentor, Earl Geiger, was retiring from Orkin. Earl had a proposition for his young protégé. They would identify a business in the right circumstances, in the right location. Harvey and Earl would each put up half of the capital. Harvey would lead the operation, and when the time was right, Harvey would buy out Earl's share of the business.

At the time, it appeared to Harvey to be a perfect plan. Their focus immediately turned south to Florida.

In early January 1985, after working hard, learning a great deal, moving himself, Carol, and his children no fewer than nine times, and preparing himself by gaining a total understanding of the residential services business over the previous twenty-two years, Harvey informed Terminix CEO Ned Cook of his decision to give up the outstanding salary, his beautiful corner office, a clear path to corporate leadership, and the security of working with a strong, independent, well-known, and well-run industry leader, in order to go out on his own.

The family was moving, for a tenth and, as things turned out, final time, to Orlando in Central Florida.

• • •

People who grew up in the 1950s and '60s know the name Lucille Ball. Although it isn't widely known, in addition to being an excellent actress and comedienne, Ms. Ball was a savvy, shrewd, and experienced businesswoman. When a reporter commented on her extreme good luck late in her remarkable career in film and television, she looked him square in the eye and, paraphrasing the Roman philosopher Seneca, replied, "Luck is when, after a whole lot of hard work, one recognizes, seizes, and makes the very best of an opportunity."

It's fair to suggest Harvey Massey would have been successful in anything he did, including the real estate business in Austin, Texas, and on the corporate side of the residential and commercial services business with either Orkin or Terminix. It's also fair to suggest that had that Austin real estate broker at Harrison, Wilson, and Pearson *not* suggested Harvey go out and get a job, learn the territory, and meet as many local folks as possible, none of what occurred in his life and career following him crawling under that house in Killeen, Texas, would have happened, including this book.

Instead, Harvey clearly recognized, then seized the opportunity before him. The rest, well, that will come into considerably sharper focus over the remaining chapters of *When Your Name Is On the Door.*

Based on how things played out for him, Carol, and their three children between 1963 and 1984 and beyond, I don't think Harvey Massey would disagree with the notion that sometimes, it's okay if a plan doesn't work out as intended.

Moments and Milestones

Chapter 1: 1941–1984

- Harvey Massey grows up in Melville, Louisiana (1941–1959).
- Harvey serves in the US Army (1959–1961).
- He joins Orkin Exterminating in Austin, Texas (February 1, 1963).
- Harvey and Carol (Nisula) marry in Austin, Texas (August 24, 1963).
- Angela (Angie) is born two and a half months prematurely in Austin (March 21, 1964).
- Tony is born in San Antonio (September 10, 1966).
- Andrea is born in La Salle, Illinois (July 15, 1972).
- Harvey joins Terminix International in Memphis, Tennessee (1979).
- Harvey leaves Terminix in late 1984, purchases the Walker Chemical and Exterminating Company in Orlando, and permanently relocates to Central Florida (February 1985).

INVESTOR BUYS PEST CONTROL FIRM

Investor Harvey L. Massey has bought Orlando-based Walker Chemical & Exterminating Co. for an undisclosed price.

Walker Chemical is a pest control company, and posted 1984 sales of $4 million.

Massey was formerly executive vice president, operations, of Memphis, Tenn.-based Terminex, another pest control company. Massey will be president and chief executive officer of Walker and will relocate in Orlando.

Orlando Sentinel *Business Section, February 1985*

CHAPTER 2

The Beginning

"It's done."

After a grueling day on Wednesday, February 20, 1985, Harvey Massey returned to his room at the Mount Vernon Inn on South Orlando Avenue in Winter Park, Florida. He removed his shoes, took off his tie, and collapsed onto the bed. Harvey stared at the heavens and implored God to please bless the transaction he'd just completed at the law offices of Bogin, Munns & Munns in downtown Orlando. Then he picked up the phone and called Carol. When she answered, he said only two words.

"It's done."

He's told the story so often it's risen to legend status within the halls of Massey Services.

"With two children in college and one ready to enter high school, I went almost four million dollars into debt to acquire the Walker Chemical and Exterminating Company in Orlando, Florida," he's said more times than he can count.

But wait. Once again, this was *not* how the plan was originally conceived.

When Harvey's friend and mentor from his time at Orkin, Earl Geiger, brought the proposition of business ownership to him, it was going to be the two of them putting up the money along with Harvey's sweat equity. *That* had been the plan.

What changed? And what happened to Earl's money?

Well, despite all his best intentions, between the original conversation back in the summer of 1984 and that signing of papers in Rulon Munns's office on February 20, 1985,

due to unexpected personal and family considerations, Earl was no longer able to participate financially in the purchase of the business.

Harvey was ready to jettison the whole deal, but Earl wouldn't hear of it. He told his protégé that there was absolutely no reason he shouldn't move ahead on his own.

Earl said, "You know everything you need to know, and you have everything you need to have in order to make this happen."

Harvey had always subscribed to a quote attributed to Mark Twain: "The two most important days in your life are the day you are born and the day you find out why." By the time they'd finished discussing things, Earl Geiger had convinced Harvey Massey that he was born to own and operate his own business. Truer words had never been spoken.

"He reminded me that my sixteen years with Orkin and my six years with Terminix left me literally with everything I needed to know and understand about the business in order to be successful," Harvey said. "It wasn't as if I was buying a business without knowing what I was getting. I understood the nuts and bolts of operating a pest and termite service business. I understood the financial side. I understood management. I understood people, and I understood what's fundamentally important in business. I decided to take Earl's counsel and complete the deal alone."

A great many people are thankful that he did.

• • •

At the time of purchase, the Walker Chemical and Exterminating Company had four service centers in Central Florida. The flagship was located at 3210 Clay Avenue, near the Orlando neighborhood of College Park. It was a large, converted home housing not only Walker's Orlando service facility, but two actual residences, one of which was occupied by Mrs. Stella May Walker, the ninety-one-year-old matriarch of the business. There were additional Walker service facilities in Daytona Beach, in Rockledge, near Cocoa, and in Ft. Pierce, all of which are still multi segment locations for Massey Services.

In addition to the company's four service centers, Harvey purchased fifty-eight service vehicles, several in various stages of disrepair, and inherited the company's employees and customer base, along with land, buildings, leases, equipment, product inventory, and outstanding obligations. He learned he'd purchased a below-market pricing structure because Walker was fearful of losing customers if they raised prices to meet both revenue and profit goals and objectives, and performance standards.

Upon closer examination of the company's pen-and-ink financials, Harvey concluded that Stella May and her son, B.J. Walker, had a more casual approach to business than he did.

Stella Mae and B.J. Walker

"We had sufficient information to complete the purchase with a degree of confidence," Harvey said. "What we weren't aware of at that moment was everything we didn't know we were going to have to do to move the company forward, as it existed at the time of the acquisition."

• • •

Harvey and Carol moved their family into a suburban home in Seminole County, off Markham Woods Road in the town of Longwood, between Interstate 4 and the Wekiva River. It was, depending on traffic, a fifteen-to-thirty-minute commute to work.

"Angela was heading into graduate school at the University of Florida. Tony was an undergrad in finance at the University of Alabama, and Andrea was getting ready to enter Lake Mary High School," Harvey said. "I knew Carol would establish a lovely home for us while I worked whatever hours were necessary to get things moving at the business. Everyone we asked directed us to south Seminole County, where we'd live until we were comfortable the business was hitting on all cylinders."

Harvey was never known to be a patient man. They lived in Longwood for four years before moving to Winter Park, where they wanted to be then and where they make their home today in a house on the shore of Lake Maitland.

"Mrs. Walker and her son, B.J., had different opinions and ideas regarding the future of the company," he said. "This was one of the primary reasons the business was available for sale. Another reason involved a stagnant revenue picture. In 1983 and 1984, Walker generated almost the same annual revenues: $3.9 million."

Harvey Massey has always been comfortable rolling around in numbers. He knew, almost immediately, that Walker had been pricing its services below what he suspected the market would bear. The first change he made—after tightening productivity efficiency and effectiveness—was to boost prices by up to 40 percent on new business. There was pushback by the existing sales force, of course, but Harvey was undeterred.

"I explained that they—our people—couldn't expect to make a better living if we were giving our services away," he said. "You also can't manage expenses if you're not maximizing a technician's time in front of a customer." This concept—limiting a technician's travel time while increasing his or her time in the presence of a customer—was and still is a crucial objective in service center management.

It was important for the people delivering the services to understand from day one that the new ownership was going to do things differently, and that if they bought into Harvey's formula for providing services more effectively and efficiently, they and the company would generate more revenue and more profit. And that meant every technician on every route would make more money. Most important to his employees and to Harvey was the reality that every one of them stood to grow, whatever their own aspirations were, by doing things more effectively and efficiently.

• • •

A few months into 1985, Harvey began the process of increasing prices for existing customers on monthly pest control services and termite protection renewals so that over time, the company would be approaching consistency with what

Harvey's previous employers were charging customers in the marketplace.

He believed there were reasonable ways to justify elevating prices consistent with the competitive landscape in Central Florida, from simple service improvements to bettering interactions with technicians and sales inspectors.

"One of the important aspects involved with increasing prices on existing customers had to do with the nature of the relationship between our customers and their technicians," he said.

In the mid-1980s, the industry standard for residential pest control relied on monthly visits and application of products inside the home to control pest activity and populations. In this paradigm, customers and technicians formed real, often long-term relationships.

"Our people were going inside customers' homes and spraying inside cabinets and onto baseboards to inhibit pests from infesting a home," Harvey said. "Customers got to know their technicians. The technician, to the customer, was the personification of the company. Customers seldom interacted with management unless there was a problem, and it was always our intention for them to not experience any problems."

Almost immediately after taking ownership of Walker Chemical and Exterminating Company, Harvey was ready to put policies and procedures in place to increase service technician productivity.

"There are really only two ways to grow revenue: raise prices and increase technician productivity," he said. "Increasing productivity involves putting technicians in the presence of more customers each day, which means cutting down on travel time between service visits. This also has the effect, on an incremental basis, of lowering costs because the technician isn't burning as much fuel between customer visits. It was, and continues to be this day, an ongoing exercise in route management efficiency."

The next step to increased productivity was to reduce the amount of time the technician needed to provide the actual service to each customer.

When this change in paradigm occurred, it would result in a tectonic shift in how Harvey's company would provide pest service. It would also begin to change how business was done throughout the entire residential pest control industry.

• • •

As far as increasing prices was concerned, the first step was to raise rate card prices for new business.

"Typically, customers don't talk about what they're paying for their service with other customers," he said. "Every customer's situation is different, and new customers needed to accept the value proposition that the service was worth what we would be charging."

Harvey's mentality was centered around the belief that his was a "premium" service for an "upscale" customer.

"Walker had some multifamily business," he said, "but most of our customers lived in and owned their own single-family homes. During the sales process, our job was to convince the customer that, particularly in Florida, pest control and termite protection were not luxuries; they were necessities. This wasn't a very difficult premise for our customers to accept. We also needed them to understand that, while there were so-called 'do-it-yourself' products available, some things were better left to a professionally trained and company-certified service technician."

• • •

The company didn't change its name from Walker Chemical and Exterminating Company to Massey Services until January 1, 1987. Until then, they didn't do much marketing beyond what Walker already had in place, which was mostly telephone directory advertising.

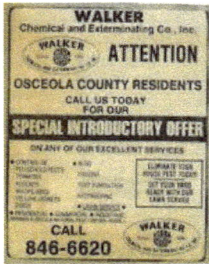

Walker Yellow Page Directory Ad

"Technicians would ask existing customers for referrals," he said, "which would make selling new business marginally easier. That said, the industry model was based on customers needing our service to address a real or perceived problem."

Pest control and termite protection were based on the perception of need as opposed to want. Harvey liked to say that no one woke up in the morning and, while drinking their coffee or eating their breakfast, decided to buy pest control services that day.

"We had a number of bridges to cross before we would be ready to invest in advertising for new business," he said. "We'd be ready to introduce ourselves to the marketplace once we'd accomplished several internal objectives."

Harvey needed to generate revenue beyond what Walker had generated in 1983 and 1984 to create the resources necessary to begin aggressively marketing for new business. This meant instilling performance standards, establishing budgets, and getting his people on his page. Part of that involved raising the current prices on Walker's existing pest control and termite protection customers. This was a somewhat delicate matter because of something called the "negative result" inherent in the business.

"Customers pay us to get rid of the problem they have," he said. "They *continue* to pay us to ensure the problem doesn't return. Sometimes, the absence of the problem leads them to believe the problem is gone. We had to dissuade them from this misconception."

Pest control and termite protection customers need to be regularly reminded that the reason they no longer have the problem they had initially is because their service technician's recurring visits prevent the problem from returning.

"If we don't do what we do, the pests are going to come back," Harvey said to his field operations force. "We need to remind our customers, all the time, that what we do, that the steps we take, keep the pests out of their homes."

Customers may not want to hear it, but the costs associated with operating a residential services business continue to escalate.

"Fuel costs; vehicle maintenance; improved, safer, more effective products; increased costs of recruiting, hiring, and developing the best people," he told his technicians, managers, and supervisors, "are the reasons we occasionally—not often, but occasionally—must marginally increase our prices."

Harvey knew customers didn't typically embrace price increases, but if the case was made by their trusted technician, as opposed to some form of cold communication—a mailed letter or a hand-delivered brochure—the information would be easier to understand and accept.

Service Technician Larry Robertson, 1987

Larry Robertson, a Walker technician in Daytona, who also worked with the Florida Highway Patrol, once told Harvey of an encounter with a customer.

"Larry told me he presented his customer, who'd been his customer for years, with a price increase from twelve dollars per visit to sixteen dollars per visit," Harvey said. "The customer told Larry she'd have to consider it because she didn't understand why the price should be raised. She even mentioned that she wasn't sure she needed to continue with the service because she wasn't experiencing any problems."

This was that "negative result" issue endemic among the industry.

"Then she told him she wanted to check with other service providers. That was the opening Larry was looking for."

One of the things Harvey learned sometime after he bought Walker was that there were more than three hundred different service providers offering essentially the same services as his company. Many of those—especially hungry, one- or two-man operations—were less costly than his already insufficiently priced services.

"Larry reminded her that he'd been visiting her home for quite a while," Harvey said. "He'd been there when she'd lost her husband to cancer. He'd been there when her daughter graduated high school and then college. Did she really want a stranger coming into her home over a few dollars per month?"

She did not, and that's what closed the deal.

• • •

The relationship between a pest service technician and their customer is different than that in almost any other industry. How many businesses are invited into the home on a monthly basis? Further, how many businesses can say their service technicians are trusted with keys and alarm codes and sometimes do their jobs when no one is at the home? When your customer trusts your service person to do what he or she says they're going to do, and then the technician delivers on that level of trust, they'll almost always want to retain that relationship rather than take a chance with someone new.

To grow, a service business must sell new business every single day, but they also need to keep every customer they already have. The only customers Harvey was willing to lose were those who moved away or those who passed away. As for the rest, he instilled in his staff the attitude that they should do everything possible and reasonable to keep the customer satisfied.

"The customer you're pursuing is important," he told them, "but the customer you already have is even more so."

• • •

Harvey Massey bought the Walker Chemical and Exterminating Company on February 20, 1985. The company had revenues of $3.9 million in 1984. They did $4.23 million in 1985, an increase of 9.22 percent. They did $4.68 million in revenue in 1986, an increase of 9 percent. These were the first two years of growth the company enjoyed even *before* becoming Massey Services in January 1987.

During this same time period, between February 20, 1985, and January 1, 1987, Harvey Massey shared with his people a couple of enduring principles he'd learned about doing business in the services sector. The first was the importance of maximizing every dollar of revenue and making sure as much as was possible that each of those dollars generated operating profit for the business. The second involved controlling expenses to the greatest extent possible, and only for those involved in growing the business and taking care of customers.

• • •

The first illustration of this was the Walker Chemical and Exterminating Company's fleet of fifty-eight vehicles. The second addressed the image of the service people employed by the company at the time.

Part of the Walker Chemical and Exterminating Company fleet

The Walker service trucks were all paid for, but they weren't even close to reaching Harvey's exacting operational and appearance standards. Harvey Massey wanted clean white vehicles with blue graphics trimmed in gold.

He also believed in leasing vehicles versus buying them.

This was an integral part of his agenda and his laser-sharp focus for transforming the company's image and, ultimately, changing its name.

In pursuit of this objective, he reached out to ARI, the vehicle leasing company with whom he'd worked at Terminix, and Cintas, the organization who handled both Orkin's and

Massey Services fleet, 1987

Terminix's service uniforms. These were two of the largest and most respected companies in their business segments. His decision to work with vendors at this level demonstrated exactly how Harvey Massey envisioned the future of the company he'd just purchased. He was using vendors he knew and who had gained his trust and confidence in the past.

Like his service vehicles, his uniforms would feature crisp white shirts emblazoned with a blue-and-white Massey Services logo. The epaulets on the shoulders were a nod to the uniforms worn by America's military services, specifically the US Army, in which he had served before joining Orkin in February 1963.

From day one, Harvey Massey imbued his employees with his ideas regarding the critical importance of a positive image. He was fond of saying, "If you don't get the look right, you'll never get the act right."

This principle extended not only to a service technician's physical appearance, including his or her cleanliness and personal grooming, but to the cleanliness and overall condition of their service vehicle and the way he or she communicated with customers.

"We always want to respond to a customer's question with a smile and a 'Yes, we can do that!' attitude," he told them. "If a customer has an unreasonable request or something out of line with our comprehensive policies and procedures, we should always respond not with 'No,' but with a 'Well, here's what we can and will do for you' approach."

In the early days, Harvey Massey took a hands-on approach to training and development. As the company grew, he trained the trainers.

• • •

As the company edged toward the official transition away from Walker and toward its new identity, Harvey went through several considerations regarding the name of the company. He elected to avoid limiting the company's potential for not only vertical, but horizontal growth in the future. He decided to call the company Massey Services, Inc.

"It wasn't because we had anything particular in mind at the time, but we didn't want to limit ourselves to just pest control and termite protection. This led us to embrace using the term 'services' as a catchall, just in case."

He knew there were some potential downsides to putting his own name on the company. In the end, though, these were not enough to deter him.

"I wasn't at all certain of much in the very beginning," he said. "I believed in myself and in the experience I'd gained with both Orkin and Terminix. I believed in the health and vibrancy of the Florida pest control and termite protection marketplace and in the industry as a whole. But there was also a great deal I wasn't yet a hundred percent certain about."

*The Massey Services logo as it appeared in 1987
and as it appears today*

Harvey decided to call the company Massey Services, Inc. not to de-emphasize what the company did, but to clean up and simplify how he'd present the company and its services to the marketplace in the future.

"There were two words in the Walker name—*chemical* and *exterminating*—that I wanted to get away from," he said. "Even then, I think I knew that repositioning exactly what we were offering to the marketplace would serve our company and our customers moving forward."

Harvey also understood there was a growing mood in the country toward environmental responsibility.

"All of our products are subject to stringent testing by both state and federal agencies for consumer safety and efficacy," he said. "By removing the words *chemical* and *exterminating* from the actual name of our company, we send a clear message to our existing and future customers about how we play in the environmental space."

• • •

Harvey Massey often reflects on the early days of his venture into ownership of his own company and the journey that was to follow when he made the decision to purchase Walker Chemical and Exterminating Company and change its name to Massey Services, Inc.

"It was, at the time, both terrifying and energizing," he said. "Terrifying because of the obligations and responsibilities. Energizing because of the enormous opportunity before us."

He may not have known where he was going, but he knew exactly what he was doing when he decided to put his name on the door. In truth, he was just getting started.

Moments and Milestones

Chapter 2: 1985–1988

- Harvey Massey purchases the Walker Chemical and Exterminating Company in Orlando, Florida for $3.9 million (February 20, 1985).
- Angie graduates from the University of Florida in Gainesville with a BA in education (1986) and a MA in speech and language pathology from the University of Mississippi in Oxford (1988).
- Gwyn Elias joins the company (1987).
- The Original Purchase:
  - » Residential, Orlando, FL
  - » Residential, Daytona Beach, FL
  - » Residential, Cocoa/Rockledge, FL
  - » Residential, Ft. Pierce, FL

Gwyn Elias, Chief Investment Officer

Massey Services – Original Purchase, Internal Expansion, Acquisitions 1985–1988

Original Purchase

1985
Residential, Orlando, FL
Residential, Daytona Beach, FL
Residential, Cocoa/Rockledge, FL
Residential, Ft. Pierce, FL

Expansion

1986
Residential, Winter Garden, FL
Residential, Port Orange, FL

1987
Residential, Ocala, FL
Residential, Oldsmar, FL
GreenUP, Orange County, FL

Acquisition

1988
Orange Park, FL
Ocala, FL
Daytona Beach, FL

*Walker Chemical and
Exterminating Company, circa
1985*

Massey Services, Inc., circa 1987

CHAPTER 3

The New Company

"There was no place to hide."

Effective January 1, 1987, the name Walker Chemical and Exterminating Company ceased to exist, and in its place, a new company called Massey Services, Inc. was born and came to life.

Having established a relationship with ARI, the leasing company Harvey worked with at Terminix, the Walker fleet of fifty-eight vehicles included in the purchase of the business were taken out of service and replaced with brand-new white service vehicles emblazoned with a bright blue Massey Services, Inc. logo.

This left Harvey with a question: "What do I do with fifty-eight trucks bearing Walker's logo in various stages of disrepair?"

Selling them wholesale would not have been worth the time and energy for someone known for his impatience. Besides, Harvey had more pressing business. He was immersed in resuscitating and building what had been a stagnant organization two short years earlier into something that would, three years down the road, begin to revolutionize the entire pest control industry.

"The idea from the get-go was to turn that inventory of vehicles into as much cash as possible," he said. "I believed there were men everywhere who, when their son or daughter reached driving age, would want to present that young man or woman with their first truck—a used one!"

There are thoughts, ideas, words, and phrases that will appear on the pages of this book repeatedly. They are part and parcel of the DNA coursing through Harvey Massey. One of those ideas has to do with image, which will be discussed later in *When Your Name Is On the Door.*

"We owned all fifty-eight of these vehicles outright," he said. "We had to keep them insured. We had to keep them registered to our company unless and until we were able to sell them and move them off our property."

An image-conscious executive like Harvey Massey decided to, in short order, clean 'em up and move 'em out.

A Walker holdover employee lived in one of the two apartments on the Clay Avenue property. Serendipitously, he was part of Walker's vehicle maintenance operation. Harvey had a deal for him.

"I told him that if he'd get every one of those vehicles in working condition and as cleaned up as possible, I'd let him put a For Sale sign on each of the dashboards and pay him a percentage of every one he sold."

Done. On to the next.

• • •

There was a particular day in early 1987 when the sign on the front lawn at 3210 Clay Avenue was changed from Walker to Massey. It was the first physical manifestation of Harvey literally putting his name on the door of his business for better or for worse and for the world to see.

"For over a half century," Harvey said, "this business was called the Walker Chemical and Exterminating Company. Just to provide a little bit of context—as of now, it's been called Massey Services for just over thirty-five years."

So, how did he feel about that? What was going through his mind at that moment?

"I was feeling a couple of different things," he said. "First, I saw it as a potential point of differentiation. It was a way to take what I viewed as negative words, such as *chemical* and *exterminating*, out of the conversation moving forward. It was a way to put the word *services* front and center in the mind of both existing and future customers. And it was a way of attaching the word *services* to the name *Massey*."

These are important distinctions and are reflected in how Massey Services has evolved over the years since those signs were switched out. But Harvey had other feelings as well.

"To be honest, right then, I was also feeling a little exposed," he said. "Anything that could happen, especially during the early period of transitioning from Walker to Massey, would automatically reflect on the business, on me, and potentially on my family. I don't think it's any kind of overstatement to say that I felt like, at least in a business sense, there was no place to hide."

The good news, of course, is that Harvey never needed to worry about hiding. In fact, in the not-too-distant future, his name would not only be on the door, but his face would be pretty much everywhere!

• • •

Soon after word of the name change made the rounds through the American pest control industry, Harvey was especially pleased when he received an unexpected phone call from a friend and competitor, Truly Nolen. Truly was living in Tucson, Arizona, at the time. Truly's father had started his business in Miami about three years after the Walkers had established the company that would become Massey Services in Orlando.

"[Truly] told me that changing the name of the company was one of the gutsiest calls he'd ever heard of," Harvey said. "That meant a lot because Truly Nolen Pest Control has always been one of the most visible and respected companies in our industry."

• • •

As things started taking shape for Massey Services in 1987, Harvey began giving thought to how he'd position the company in the marketplace through advertising and public relations. In the predigital age, it was common for homeowners to go directly to the Yellow Pages to find a solution to a real or perceived problem. Harvey Massey knew all about Yellow Page directory advertising from his time at Orkin and Terminix.

One of the things he quickly discovered about the Sunshine State was the sheer volume of pest control businesses operating in each community.

"In the early days of Massey Services, we really didn't have as much money as it would have taken to do it right in terms of getting our name out into the world beyond what Walker had been putting into Yellow Page directory advertising."

Harvey would soon learn the Orlando marketplace was, if not unique, then one of only a few in the country where there were multiple competing directories. This was due to the number of phone companies enfranchised to service the communities where Massey now had service centers, as well as potential opportunities for new business.

A very brief and relatively recent history of the Orlando area is probably in order.

In the early 1960s, Orlando and the rest of Central Florida away from the Atlantic coast was, to be charitable, a mostly sleepy citrus, ranching, and agricultural community.

In the mid-1960s, a mysterious entity began buying up acreage about twenty miles southwest of downtown Orlando near where Florida's Turnpike and Interstate 4 share an interchange. That entity, of course, turned out to be the Walt Disney Company.

The construction of Disney's first theme park, Magic Kingdom, and surrounding commercial development foretold what was to come. Once the first park opened fifty years ago, bringing thousands of jobs and new residents, Central Florida began to boom and hasn't stopped booming since.

Beginning in 1971, Orlando and the rest of Central Florida enjoyed an explosion of development, much of it to the north and east of the Disney-fueled tourism corridor. As the world now knows, southwest Orlando came to include SeaWorld, Universal Orlando, approximately 130,000 hotel rooms, and the housing and business infrastructure necessary to support all of what went into making Central Florida the number one tourism destination in the entire world.

This was the wave Harvey Massey caught in the mid-1980s, and it hasn't ever crested.

• • •

By the time he was promoted to regional vice president at Orkin, Harvey had learned that using telephone directory advertising to grow a residential services business was a costly and sometimes frustrating exercise. On the other hand, it was a proven and workable strategy.

"A lot of young people don't remember a time before cell phones," he said. "The joke we told ourselves was, a woman saw an insect crawling on the floor of the kitchen. She immediately picked up a Yellow Page telephone directory, killed the bug with it, and then called one of the pest control companies listed inside the directory."

What he didn't say when telling the joke was that at that time, in 1987, there were approximately three hundred names listed under the *Pest Control* heading in the Southern Bell version of the Orlando Yellow Page telephone directory. And that was just one of the books serving the Orlando market.

"In those early days, the directory publishers understood the leverage they had over businesses when it came to customers with real or perceived immediate needs," he said. "In the customer's mind, they either couldn't wait to ask a neighbor for a referral, or they were embarrassed at having a pest-related problem to solve. They also couldn't wait until they happened to come across a radio or television commercial. They needed a response to their problem right then and there. The fastest way to do that was to use the directory and make a choice. Now, of course, we have the internet, Google, and social media."

While Yellow Page directory advertising was costly and frustrating, Harvey concluded that it worked in creating new business opportunities in the pest control and termite protection segments. In the early days of Massey Services, it was *the* form of advertising in which he had confidence and with which he had experience, and despite all the changes in the world of communication, and although its influence has diminished when compared to brand advertising and digital direct response advertising, Yellow Page advertising remains a part of the Massey Services marketing mix to this day.

• • •

When O. Wayne Rollins promoted Harvey to vice president of their Midwest region, Orkin's chairman was skeptical about what he viewed as major northern cities, such as Chicago, Minneapolis, Detroit, and Cleveland.

"He wasn't sure there was enough demand in some of the larger, colder locations," Harvey said. "It required some research, but I was of the opinion that for the customer we would be targeting—the middle-to-upper-middle-class, single-family homeowner—both residential pest control and termite protection were still essential services."

That certainty and that mindset would follow Harvey Massey throughout his career.

He visited each midwestern location and rode with service technicians, service managers, and branch managers to get the lay of the land and see for himself where those customers lived. He outlined neighborhoods, villages, towns, and entire counties where most of the population constituted his target customers.

"Customers looking for our services wanted to work with local businesses," he said. "They wanted us to be where they were. Said differently, they wanted us close by."

In fact, customers responded to the illusion of proximity. This meant employing a subtle but unique marketing strategy involving telephone exchanges. In the pre-cell phone era, when residential calls sometimes involved a toll charge, it was Harvey's position that by removing that impediment, potential customers would be more inclined to make those calls. He was right.

"We asked the phone companies to sell us a service that would create the customer impression that, by calling what they viewed as a 'local' number, they were obtaining their service from a local service provider."

He implemented this strategy in one location after another, throughout Orkin's Midwest region. Everywhere he did it, business growth followed. Even before he was done, Mr. Rollins brought Harvey and his family back to Atlanta, placing him in charge of Orkin's central region, the company's crown jewel.

Massey Services Yellow Page Directory Ad

This was how, after changing the company's name from Walker to Massey but before opening additional service centers—which would occur when he'd sufficiently begun to penetrate new market areas—Harvey Massey began growing Massey Services. He did it using Yellow Page directory advertising featuring multiple different telephone numbers targeting specific neighborhoods and areas but without toll charges for his future customers.

Suffice it to say, his strategy worked.

• • •

It's not to be known whether Harvey Massey's approach to growing Massey Services was either to emulate or radically turn away from either of the industry giants with whom he had worked. He freely acknowledges the influence of both Orkin and Terminix on how he structured some of his internal policies, procedures, and processes.

"It's never instructive to believe that by going out on your own, you're repudiating everything you learned somewhere else," he said. "These companies didn't become who they are by accident."

Neither would Massey Services.

His general managers and services managers handled the day-to-day jobs associated with growing the business and servicing the company's customers, while Harvey spent a considerable amount of his time identifying where the company would begin the process of growth through internal expansion. At this point in time, with Massey Services still in its relative toddler years, Harvey was getting to know the lay of the land in the Metro Orlando counties—Orange, Seminole, and Osceola—as well as in Daytona and DeLand in Volusia County, Cocoa and Rockledge in Brevard County, and along the Treasure Coast of Florida, from Vero Beach in Indian River County to Ft. Pierce in St. Lucie County, as well as Martin County.

With existing service centers already in place, Harvey had his eye on making deeper penetration into the company's current marketplaces before stepping out into the rest of what, at the time, was the fastest growing state in the United States.

"There are two ways to grow," Harvey often said. "First, there's internal expansion. Then, there's acquisition."

There's much more about growth coming up in *When Your Name Is On the Door.*

• • •

In the mid-1980s, Central Florida was still experiencing its own huge internal expansion, fueled by the opening of Magic Kingdom at Walt Disney World in 1971. Disney's Magic Kingdom was just the first ladder step in the meteoric growth of Central Florida. It was followed by the arrival of SeaWorld in 1973, EPCOT at Walt Disney World in 1982, Disney-MGM Studios (now Disney's Hollywood Studios) in 1989, and Universal Orlando in 1990. Disney's Animal Kingdom and Universal's Islands of Adventure would follow.

All these tourism destinations meant more hotels, more apartment complexes, more single-family subdivisions, and more hospitality and retail businesses to support the new visitors and residents living in and visiting Metro Orlando.

All this represented opportunity for Massey Services.

In 1981, Orlando International Airport opened, making a major statement in domestic and international air travel away from its clunky predecessor, Orlando Jetport at McCoy Air Force Base. Today, Orlando International Airport—MCO as it is known in the airline industry—is the point of arrival for over 50 million visitors to the Orlando tourism and business corridor every year.

This explosion of tourism, which really began in 1965 with notice of Disney's intentions and investment, impacted the Orlando metropolitan area (Orange, Seminole, and Osceola Counties) enormously. In 1965, the tri-county area had a resident population of 250,000. In 1985, when Harvey Massey purchased the Walker Chemical and Exterminating Company, that same tri-county area was home to nearly three times the 1965 population, or 723,000 people.

Since then, the marketplace has continued to grow at no less than 2 to 3 percent per year. At the publication of this book, the population of Metro Orlando will exceed two million people!

• • •

Massey Services hit the ground at full throttle and has stayed there since arriving on January 1, 1987.

"There really was no time for us to reflect on the environment in which we were operating," Harvey acknowledges today. "The growth that was occurring everywhere in Florida was fueled by what was happening in Central Florida. Daytona was the 'World's Most Famous Beach,' Cocoa-Rockledge was home to the American space program, and the Ft. Pierce and Port St. Lucie area was evolving into one of the first major middle- and upper-middle-class retirement communities in the eastern United States."

In Harvey Massey's world, every single one of the folks in each of those communities lived and worked in a house or commercial building somewhere that needed both pest control and termite protection.

• • •

Before 1987 came to an end, Harvey opened GreenUP Lawn, Tree and Shrub Care as a separate business segment from pest control and termite protection. This was a logical extension for Massey Services. In addition, the company opened pest control and termite protection business units in Ocala and Oldsmar,

Florida. In 1988, Massey Services expanded by adding pest control and termite protection service centers in Orange Park, Florida, and acquired J.F. Porter in Ocala, Doty Exterminating in Daytona Beach, and Porter Pest Control in Orange Park.

• • •

There were anywhere from dozens to hundreds of competing businesses occupying the space under the *Pest Control* heading in the dozen or more Yellow Page directories serving the Florida communities where Massey Services was engaged in the establishment of a competitive beachhead. Many, like Massey Services, were buying full- and three-quarter-page ads, and more than half of those listings began with letters that came before M, giving them a slight advantage in an alphabetically structured advertising medium.

Full-page ads were positioned in each directory based on when the ad was first placed, meaning people had to sweep by large-scale ads from Massey's competitors before getting their first look at what Massey Services had to offer. Customers tended to assume that bigger ads meant more successful companies who were better than their competitors.

"If a potential customer moved into one of the communities we were serving," Harvey said, "there was a chance they'd already have a regional or national preference. Massey Services needed to encourage those customers to bypass their existing reference points."

• • •

In 1987, Harvey began evaluating marketing services companies to help Massey Services make the best possible investments in getting the company's name before the customer and giving the customer a reason to seek out Massey's contact information before their competitors'.

"I wasn't really sure who or what I was looking for," Harvey said. "We met with a few small-to-midsized firms with roots in Central Florida and relied on referrals and intuition."

It didn't take him long to find the right marketing services partner. As was the case with Harvey's own entry into business in Central Florida, Todd Persons Communications formed in 1985. The firm, while focused on public relations and marketing communication materials, was also extremely well connected in the community, and had in-house media buying capability.

Agency CEO Todd Persons had worked as Orlando mayor Bill Frederick's public information officer and director of communications. His prior experience was in print and broadcast journalism. In addition to years with the *Orlando Sentinel* daily newspaper, Todd had worked with two of the three national television network affiliates in their news departments.

Todd's vice president of public relations, Bud (Brewer) Katz, had worked in both radio and television news and public affairs in Central Florida, was an accomplished writer, and, along with Todd, was deeply rooted in the Central Florida community.

"We clicked within the first five or ten minutes we were together," Harvey said. "We were from the same generation,

Left to right: JoAnn and Todd Persons, Lynn and Bud (Brewer) Katz

which I think mattered at the time, and we knew, intuitively, that we were going to have to learn each other's businesses and grow together."

The first assignment Harvey gave the agency was to create and produce collateral materials for sales inspectors that would allow Massey Services to stand out from whatever customers might receive from competitors.

"All of the content was produced through a collaboration between Massey Services and the agency," Harvey said. "We used our own employees instead of contracting with professional models. Photography took place inside and outside the homes of actual customers. The agency wrote the copy, handled the printing, and delivered an outstanding product. We projected the image of a major national company."

Over the years, the agency became fully integrated into the Massey organization. In 1995, agency vice president Bud (Brewer) Katz became Massey's first director, then vice president of marketing. In 1997, Harvey Massey acquired the agency from Todd Persons and his partner, Carol Brinati, and in 2003 he installed Bud (Brewer) Katz as president and CEO of what was then called Massey Communications.

Andrea Massey-Farrell, SVP of Community Relations, President and CEO of Harvey and Carol Massey Foundation

Andrea Massey-Farrell joined Massey Communications in 2001. She stepped in to lead the agency in 2011 when Bud (Brewer) Katz retired.

All of this serves to demonstrate the nature of being part of or connected with an organization that lives its values and maintains relationships over long periods of time.

Over the next two to three years, a great deal of growth through both acquisition and internal expansion would establish the template for the company's rapid ascension in the communities where it did business and in the pest management industry overall. In addition, two singular pieces integral to the company's future would be added to Massey Services. One was a person. The other was a revolutionary game changer of an idea.

The future was about to reveal itself, and both Massey Services and the entire pest control industry was about to experience major change.

Moments and Milestones

Chapter 3: 1989–1992

- Tony graduates from the University of Alabama in Tuscaloosa and joins Massey Services (1989).
- Angie and Shane Rignanese marry in Winter Park, Florida (1990).

Left to right: Tony, Carol, Harvey, and Jann Stockman at the University of Alabama in 1988.

Angela and Shane Rignanese, 1990

- Rick Beard joins the company (1990).
- Adam Jones joins the company (1991).

Adam Jones, VP of Quality Assurance

Rick Beard, VP of Commercial Services

- Massey Services establishes its award-winning 401(k) program for the benefit of its team members.
- The company receives an advertising award of merit from the National Pest Control Association (NPCA) in 1992.

NPCA Award of Advertising Merit, 1992

- Barbara Corino joins the company (1989).
- Ed Dougherty joins the company (1992).

Ed Dougherty, EVP, COO

Barbara Corino, VP and Corporate Secretary

- Harvey Massey receives the Industry Leadership Award from ICI American and *Pest Control Technology* magazine (1992).

MASSEY SERVICES – INTERNAL EXPANSION, ACQUISITIONS 1989–1992

EXPANSION

1989
Residential, Leesburg, FL

1991
Commercial, Orlando, FL

1992
New Construction, Orlando, FL
Residential, Lake Mary, FL

ACQUISITION

1989
Leesburg, FL

1990
Eustis, FL
Zephyrhills, FL

CHAPTER 4

The Early Years

"How you say things matters. Words matter."

By the end of the 1980s, Massey Services was moving along in a comfortable, controlled pattern of growth. Revenues were up, as were profits. Customer count was rising, along with the number of team members required to service those customers. But at least one person—the most important one—was not yet comfortable.

"I learned a long time ago, back in the early 1990s, from a very, very smart man, that there never has been, there is not now, and there never will be a business model that is permanent," Harvey said, quoting Professor Ben Shapiro of Harvard Business School. "There are probably as many business models in America as there are businesses. I haven't put a whole lot of thought into the subject, but it seems that if we had a specific business model, ours would be to grow every year in a measured fashion, to take the best possible care of every one of our customers and team members, to conservatively manage the financial side of all our business units, and to build a bench for the future."

At the end of 1987, just a few months shy of two years since his purchase of the Walker Chemical and Exterminating Company, Harvey decided to get into the lawn care business. The lawn, tree, and shrub care marketplace shared a lot of connective tissue with the pest control and termite protection segments, to which Massey Services was already committed.

"While this wasn't a complete stretch for us," he said, "there weren't many pest and termite companies moving into the space. Most of our competition would be from companies solely in lawn and landscape care."

Harvey had more than just a bit of trepidation about the notion of getting into this segment. In fact, more than once, he'd indicated he really didn't care much for the residential lawn care business.

"It's a product-intensive business," he said. "Orkin tried the lawn care business. It didn't work for them, so they ultimately sold it to Terminix. At the time, those companies were all over the country. For much of the American pest industry, lawn care was seen as seasonal. We were in Florida, and in Florida, it made more sense."

It's important to make a clear distinction between Harvey's idea of lawn care and what the words themselves might connote. Massey Services, through its newly formed lawn, tree, and shrub care segment, would not be offering customers lawn mowing, trimming, and edging services, but would instead provide treatments with products designed to enhance the health and appearance of a homeowner's lawn and landscape. In fact, the advertising tagline developed for marketing lawn services would one day be "Enhancing the Beauty of Nature."

Ultimately, Harvey decided to brand lawn, tree, and shrub

care services separately from offerings in pest control and termite protection, but there was sufficient connectivity between the services that a commitment to this segment seemed appropriate. Harvey planted his flag for this venture on GreenUP Lawn, Tree and Shrub Care. Years later, in 2007, the division added irrigation system maintenance to its portfolio and changed the nomenclature to "landscape services."

Early GreenUP logo, circa 1988

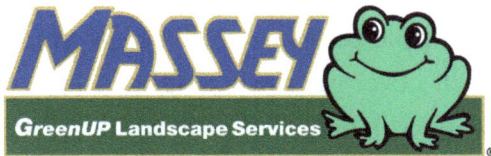

GreenUP Landscape Services logo, circa 2010

"Many of the fertilization and insect control products came from the same manufacturers and wholesalers we worked with in pest control and termite protection," he said. "The equipment necessary to provide the services was similar. There were similarities and differences in exactly how the services were sold and performed, but the fact that we had a sizable, built-in customer base from which to initially draw made entry into the business of landscape services a simple affirmative decision."

A major competitor in the lawn and landscape care business turned out to be a company named ChemLawn, which, at the time, was wholly owned by ServiceMaster, the parent of Terminix, the company Harvey Massey left to establish his own place in the industry.

Harvey tells a story about jogging along Markham Woods Road in Longwood quite early one morning when he noticed a ChemLawn service truck parked in front of a home in a nearby upscale subdivision.

"I recall it was a good-looking vehicle," he said. "Clean and well equipped. I saw their tech working on a very good-looking lawn. He looked sharp. This gave me some ideas about our own people."

When he arrived at his office that morning, he held a brief meeting. "I told everyone what I saw and when I saw it. I let them know that when you start earlier, you look better. When you look better, you're going to be better."

It was an example of that corollary, "If you don't get the look right, you'll never get the act right." Harvey also made a connection around that time which would, down the road a bit, bear important fruit.

"I called the ChemLawn service center," he said. "I wanted to let them know I appreciated the early morning service, the clean vehicle, and the sharp-looking technician." The service center manager was a young man named Rick Beard. "Rick and I had a good conversation. I told him that someday he would probably come to what I like to call a 'career crossroad' and that he should hang on to my phone number, and I would do the same."

It wasn't much further down the road when Harvey's recommendation turned into Rick Beard joining Massey Services near the end of 1990. Save for a short hiatus, Rick has been in various leadership slots within the company and today serves as vice president for Massey's commercial services division.

Harvey Massey came to accept the notion that the lawn is the canvas upon which the house is painted. He has often said—and taught—that unlike in the pest and termite businesses, a person's lawn is a visual indicator of things. One of those was whether that home might also be a candidate for Massey's GreenUP services.

"First of all, if the lawn doesn't appear healthy, if there are brown or dead spots, there's an opportunity for us. It's also beneficial to know if the home is already being serviced by us for pest control or termite protection. That makes a sale an easier proposition."

• • •

One of the reasons Harvey put his own name on the company he'd purchased was that Walker had the word *chemical* in its name.

Discussing ChemLawn, he said, "Even though many of the products we use are, in fact, chemical compositions, in the public's mind, the word *chemical* can come with a negative connotation. Our division—at that point, not yet branded—is in the lawn and landscape *care* business, not in the application of *chemicals* on a customer's lawn business."

The first of the company's lawn, tree, and shrub care customers would come from Massey's Clay Avenue service center in Orlando.

"We already had a few thousand pest control and termite renewal customers at our Clay Avenue service center," Harvey said. "We prepared a door-hanger brochure specifically for them, which allowed us to manage cost per lead and cost per sale. It also gave us the ability to carefully establish our internal controls for product usage and service procedures."

The company developed a language for the lawn care business that would further position it separately from Massey's pest control and termite protection services. Instead of service technicians, services would be provided by lawn specialists, who would be trained to provide service specifically to GreenUP customers.

• • •

In June 1991, Harvey broke out the commercial business the company inherited from Walker, as well as what had been developed by Massey Services since the acquisition. It was called, inside the company, Massey Commercial Pest Control.

"We were operating in what had already become the number one tourism destination in America, if not the world," Harvey said. "At the time, there were over eighty thousand hotel rooms in Metro Orlando and thousands of small and large, independent and chain restaurants. We already had a small book of business outside the residential services space. I felt it was time to pay more focused attention to the commercial business."

Massey Commercial Services grew alongside the residential business. It was a much more price-sensitive segment, required a different level of training, some specialized products, and an elevated approach to sales. Mostly though, it meant making the commitment to provide service on a twenty-four-hours-a-day, seven-days-a-week schedule and staffing for those service requirements.

"Much of what was required by commercial customers caused us to expand our thinking about when and how we'd take care of business for them," Harvey said. "It also provided a mechanism for us to move into new geographical areas, since many of our customers had locations in places where we weren't providing residential services at the time. Technicians were always encouraged to keep an eye out for new service opportunities. They'd be compensated for bringing in new business, and we'd be a little bit closer to opening a new service center."

• • •

This was all a part of Harvey Massey's strategy in segmenting the company's business units. By narrowing the scope of a business unit—residential pest and termite, lawn and landscape services, and commercial pest—and keeping management laser focused on a particular service segment and the eyes of his service folks trained on a single customer type, his people would become more expert in their field and provide service more confidently to Massey's customers. It was, in Harvey's view, a classic win-win situation.

• • •

For almost anyone involved with Massey Services over the past thirty years or so, the end of 1989 marked the moment when the long-term future of the company's leadership took root.

Tony Massey was on the brink of graduating from the University of Alabama with a degree in corporate finance and investment management. He'd originally planned to take that degree to Atlanta or some other major southern financial center and get into banking. This was yet another plan—this time on the part of yet another guy named Massey—that didn't work out the way it was originally formulated.

About three weeks before his graduation, Tony called his father and invited him up to Tuscaloosa for a football game. Harvey had told him he'd have to check with his mother.

"He said to me, 'You know, Dad, maybe this time you should come alone.'"

Harvey smiled when he recounted this story.

"All I could think of at the time was, what kind of trouble is he in that, three weeks before graduation, he wants me to come for a visit alone?"

When Harvey arrived in Tuscaloosa, he was relieved to learn his only son had not gotten into any sort of trouble. Instead, Tony was having second thoughts about what he would do following graduation.

During summer breaks from high school in the Memphis suburb of Germantown and from college in Tuscaloosa, Tony Massey had worked as a service technician for Terminix International in both pest control and termite protection. It was a safe bet in most quarters that at some point in time, he'd turn toward Massey Services, just not right out of school.

"I'd always wanted him to get some experience with another company," Harvey said, no doubt recalling the advice a real estate broker in Austin gave him nearly a quarter century earlier when he was just twenty-two years old.

Tony Massey had a different idea.

"I told him that I wanted to come to work at Massey Services," Tony said.

"I told him that if this was really what he wanted to do, he'd do it like any other entry-level team member like I did it, from the ground up," Harvey said.

"I said I expected that would be the case," Tony said. "I was ready."

Armed with a degree in banking, finance, and investments that offered absolutely nothing in the way of education or background in the pest control, termite protection, and landscape services business, Tony Massey joined what officially became, with his arrival, the family business.

"It's obviously easy to say with thirty years of hindsight, but Tony took to the business immediately," Harvey said. "I know he was concerned about his last name and about his youth when compared with the people he'd be working with. It never really became an issue."

Tony Massey entered a comprehensive, intense, year-long rotational training program designed expressly for someone in his unique circumstances. He was Harvey and Carol's only son, and while their youngest daughter, Andrea, would join the company years later, it would not involve her working in a Massey Services operational position. There will be more about Andrea Massey-Farrell and her roles later in *When Your Name Is On the Door*.

Before he went anywhere in the field, Tony consumed every company operational policy, procedure, and process. He studied the financials, Massey's personnel policies, its vehicle operation policies, and all service center and corporate administrative processes.

Working alongside experienced professionals with years, sometimes decades, of experience, Tony wore the uniform and did the exact same tasks as every other Massey Services pest and termite technician and lawn specialist. He put in time as a sales inspector in all three residential segments: pest prevention, termite protection, and lawn, tree, and shrub care, as well as in commercial pest control. He shadowed service managers and general managers for several months before circulating through the company's corporate human resources and finance operations.

Finally, he was assigned to manage a small, relatively new, struggling service center the company had opened in Kissimmee about twenty miles southwest of Orlando. In the Harvey L. Massey management tradition, Tony was given basically one charge: grow the business!

He did that, plus a whole lot more since asking his father to come to Tuscaloosa that December afternoon back in 1989 to discuss his future.

From that first day following graduation and for nearly a year after, Tony Massey worked in the field in residential and commercial services. He moved into the corporate finance department in 1992 and into the personnel department until 1994, when, just shy of his twenty-eighth birthday, he assumed the position of regional manager for Massey's South Florida service centers. In 1995, he added Massey's commercial division, and in 1998, he was named vice president of the central region. He was thirty-two, the same age his father was when he was named Orkin's youngest vice president.

In 1999, he added Massey's Georgia and new construction divisions to his portfolio. In 2002, Tony was promoted again, this time to executive vice president for operations, covering all of Massey's consumer services. In January 2005, he became executive vice president and chief operating officer, and in

September 2006, the father passed part of the torch to the son, when Tony Massey was named president and chief operating officer of Massey Services.

"I'm extremely proud of the man, the husband and father, the community citizen, and the business executive Tony has become," Harvey said.

One could be forgiven for wondering if, like his father, Tony wasn't born to do this.

• • •

Harvey Massey never regretted not going to college after being honorably discharged from the US Army Security Agency nearly twenty-four years before officially launching Massey Services. He did, however, soak up every bit of knowledge about business, which led him to take advantage of the opportunity to pursue the Owner/President Management program (OPM) at Harvard Business School.

"There are programs available from some of the most outstanding and prestigious business schools in America," Harvey said. "I could have attended similarly focused opportunities at Stanford, Duke, the Darden School at the University of Virginia, but when you have the chance to go to Harvard, you go!"

More than once, Harvey would take a group of company executives up to Harvard for a weekend seminar series. During one such visit in 1998, one of those executives, somewhat overwhelmed by his surroundings, told Harvey that he felt smarter just by walking around the Harvard campus.

"Each August, for the three years from 1990 through 1992, I joined approximately eighty executives from nearly two dozen countries around the world for three intensive weeks in Cambridge, Massachusetts," Harvey said. "It was one of the most important learning experiences I ever had and one I was pleased to share with others from Massey Services and with other executives both inside and outside the industry."

The requirements for entry— besides a rather steep tuition—include a proven business leadership track record over at least ten years, a personal referral from a graduate, and a willingness to check one's ego at the door. When he talks about his time at Harvard, Harvey is always very clear that this program was not a social event.

"Virtually every day, our class examined three to four case studies involving both successful businesses and some that stumbled, for one reason or another," he said. "We also received what I've come to realize was a crash course in the American capitalistic economic system."

By the end of his three-year commitment at Harvard, in line with his belief that people must never stop learning, Harvey Massey began sending senior executives to advanced management and leadership programs throughout the nation in 1992.

"We're always looking for new, often better, ideas that will help us improve our image and our performance," he said.

He also began contributing to educational initiatives in Central Florida, including significant support to Junior Achievement, the worldwide nonprofit organization dedicated to teaching K–12 students how to succeed in the global economy.

In furtherance of his father's ongoing commitment to education, Tony Massey completed Harvard's Key Executive program in 2000, and he received an Executive MBA at the Crummer Graduate School of Business at Rollins College in Winter Park, Florida, in 2012.

• • •

In the middle to later part of 1990, Harvey's company was about to complete its sixth year of growth in both annual revenue and operating profit, fully doubling the $3.9 million Walker had generated in 1983 and 1984. He brought together the Massey Services operational leadership team, including his son, Tony; his CFO, Gwyn Elias; Elizabeth Duggan, newly hired as director of administration; and his agency team, including Bud (Brewer) Katz and Todd Persons, to talk shop, as he put it at the time.

The company's first television and radio advertising campaign in the Orlando, Daytona, and Cocoa marketplace had been low-key and focused mainly on the theme of trust. There will be more about trust in the next chapter of *When Your Name Is On the Door*.

The ad copy drove people to their Yellow Page directories, and Harvey surrendered to everyone's belief that he was the best possible spokesperson for the company as opposed to a bland voice-over. He appeared and offered the close in each thirty-second television commercial.

The shoptalk took place at the Massey Services training facility down the hall from Harvey's office. Massey's corporate facility was, at the time, situated in Maitland Center, an office park located about seven miles from the Clay Avenue service centers. The conversation evolved into a brainstorm about pest control. Despite having toiled in the industry for nearly twenty-eight years, Harvey expressed some frustration with the idea—or rather the words themselves: pest *control*.

"There were hundreds of companies throughout Central Florida in the pest control business," he said. "I didn't want Massey Services lumped together with one-man operations who didn't do what we do or project what we represent in the industry."

He was talking about his company's image and its commitment to customers and team members. Vestiges of the Walker Chemical and Exterminating Company had been virtually forgotten by then. The company still operated out of service facilities Harvey had purchased from Walker, but that, along with a handful of Walker people, was about all that was left.

In matters involving how the company would craft its image in the future, in both the marketplace and within the industry and communities, words became important. Safe, effective product application could only accomplish so much. Unsanitary conditions, faulty construction, and a variety of other possible scenarios all impact a company's ability to keep pests from penetrating a structure.

"We can't and we won't promise things we're unable to control and therefore unable to deliver," he said, referring to the fact that Massey Services—or any other company in the pest control industry—couldn't in good conscience tell customers they'd never see an ant, roach, or spider inside their homes.

Harvey explained, for the benefit of the nonoperational people in the room, exactly how sales inspectors sold Massey's services and how technicians and specialists delivered those services. He explained how the industry had been moving away from using the words *pest control* and gravitating instead toward *pest management* for years. But he wasn't thrilled with those words either.

"How we say things matters," he said. "Words matter. We don't want to control pests, and we don't want to manage them either."

A whole lot of thoughts were expressed in the room in an attempt identify how to separate Massey Services from the pack. Harvey perked up when one of those in attendance uttered the word "prevention." He'd had similar thoughts over the years.

"Our program, with a few relatively minor modifications, is actually already aimed at *pest prevention*," he said. "We still can't account for the customer's role in helping keep pests out of their homes, but we can focus attention on what we are able to do."

The conversation moved to how Massey Services would teach pest control professionals already steeped in the industry tradition of spraying baseboards and kitchen and bathroom cabinets to service the property outside to keep the pests out.

The marketing people attached the word *premium* to pest prevention, and a brand-new, precedent-setting service model was born. It was called Premium Pest *Prevention* from Massey Services. That word, *premium*, would fade away because of concerns about the potential for mistaken customer impressions regarding price. The tagline became "Massey prevents pests from getting inside in the first place, so we won't have to control or manage them later."

The differentiation Harvey was looking for had arrived.

The same principles didn't apply to the termite side of the business for several reasons, but that segment would undergo its own evolution in coming years with the arrival of perimeter baiting and wood treatment products and programs.

By the end of 1990, Massey Services had acquired small businesses in Leesburg, Eustis, and Zephyrhills, Florida. Barbara Corino joined the company as Harvey's executive secretary and would, in 1997, be named vice president and corporate secretary. As mentioned earlier, Rick Beard had also arrived. The company would end the year with revenues of $8.5 million, up 15.9 percent over the 30.2 percent jump in 1989.

• • •

Ahead, two enormously significant initiatives, with impacts both inside the company and in the national pest management marketplace, would supercharge the next chapter of Harvey's and Massey Services' amazing story in the American structural pest management industry.

Moments and Milestones

Chapter 4: 1993–1996

- Angie and Shane Rignanese welcome their daughter Kallie (1993) and their daughter Ashley (1995).
- Tony and Jann Stockman marry in Tuscaloosa, Alabama (1994), and welcome their son Sean (1996).

Jann and Tony Massey, 1994

- Harvey Massey receives the Leadership Award from Zeneca Professional Products (1993) and the Service to Mankind Award from the Leukemia Society of Central Florida (1994).
- Bud (Brewer) Katz joins the company (1995).
- Massey Services wins PLCAA's 1995 Community Service Award for sponsorship of Earth Day.

Bud (Brewer) Katz, 1995

MASSEY SERVICES – INTERNAL EXPANSION, ACQUISITIONS 1993–1997

EXPANSION

1993

Residential, Kissimmee, FL
Residential, Oviedo, FL
GreenUP, Oviedo, FL

1994

Commercial, Daytona Beach, FL

1995

GreenUP, Daytona Beach, FL
Residential, DeLand, FL
Residential, Melbourne, FL
Residential, Jacksonville, FL

1996

Commercial, Boca Raton, FL
GreenUP, Osceola County, FL
GreenUP, Marion County, FL

ACQUISITION

1994

Naples, FL

Mission Statement

Guiding Philosophy

This We Believe:

◆ Above all, we are committed to *TOTAL CUSTOMER SATISFACTION*.

◆ We believe in building *LONG-TERM, TRUSTING RELATIONSHIPS* with *Customers* and *Team Members*.

◆ We value *TRUTH* and *INTEGRITY*.
Never compromise! Be consistent and fair.

◆ We are committed to *ONGOING TRAINING* and *TEAM MEMBER EDUCATION* which develop pride, job enrichment, and personal and professional growth.

◆ We believe *"OUR PEOPLE MAKE THE DIFFERENCE."*
Knowing that our future rests squarely on the work ethic, image, knowledge, imagination, skills, dependability, and integrity of our team members, we respect and value these qualities most highly.

◆ We value *OUR COMPANY'S IMAGE*.
The public perception of our team members, vehicles, equipment, and materials is essential to our success.

◆ We are committed to *INNOVATION* and *CREATIVITY* to produce safer, more efficient and effective technologies and methods.

◆ We believe in being a *CONTRIBUTING* member to our Community and Industry.

◆ We value *TEAMWORK*; think *WE* and *US*!

◆ We are committed to *GROWTH WITH PROFIT* and believe this provides the greatest assurance of security and promotional opportunities for each team member.

Our Purpose

To provide beneficial services that protect health, food, property and the quality of our environment.

Mission

Massey Services will be the leader in providing an environmentally responsible and superior service. Our Company will grow by adhering to the highest standards of performance and professionalism. Our ultimate goal is to be recognized as the best service company in our industry.

Harvey L. Massey,
Chairman & Chief Executive Officer

CHAPTER 5

Trust and Confidence

"It's about creating a satisfied customer."

One of the important elements in the relationship between Massey Services and its fast-growing customer base was the individual customer's sense of trust.

"We want every one of our customers to trust Massey Services," Harvey said. "We need to convey, in our marketing materials, in our advertising, in all of our customer communication, but mostly between our people and the people they serve, that we can be trusted to do what we say we are going to do."

This became an ongoing theme in every aspect of field training. Harvey wasn't interested in playing with words or simply asking for the customer's trust. He wanted to be as clear as possible to avoid misunderstandings, and he wanted to draw a distinction and connection between two words he felt were imperative in communicating with customers. Those words were *trust* and *confidence*.

"It's important that customers feel respected. It's important they know that their concerns, if they have them, are being addressed and that we are going to meet our commitments to them," he said. "It's a relatively simple concept, but in terms of both perception and reality, it's also not easy to deliver."

The relationship between a customer and a service provider is almost always a tenuous one. The customer has wants, needs, and expectations. The service provider, in almost every instance, has competition ready to pounce if any of those aren't met—even once. The service provider must be able to meet the customer's wants, needs, and expectations. This is an issue of confidence.

"It's essential that the customer have confidence that we *can* do what we say we're going to do," Harvey said. "It's of equal importance, alongside accepting our ability to do what we say we're going to do, that the customer trusts us when we say we *will* do it!"

One word, *confidence*, has to do with ability. The other word, *trust*, has to do with intent.

"There are a lot of examples of unkept promises in the service industry," he said. "Simply saying what you intend to do doesn't mean you're able to deliver on that promise. Conversely, simply being able to do what you say you're going to do doesn't mean you will actually do it."

Harvey Massey made it a point to always teach his sales inspectors the wisdom of under promising and overdelivering.

"By managing a customer's expectations, which is the most difficult of the three—wants, needs, and expectations—you will almost always be able to keep them satisfied," he said. "In other words, once we have created an environment where the customer understands what we can and what we cannot do, by doing what we say we are going to do, we are better able to create what every service provider seeks: a satisfied customer."

• • •

At a meeting of his corporate staff, general managers, service managers, and others, including technical specialists and his marketing people, Harvey held court on the notion of how to best keep customers satisfied with Massey Services.

In the early 1990s, no company Harvey knew of in the pest control, termite protection, or lawn care segments offered anything resembling a money-back guarantee. Massey Services was no exception. Customers aren't interested in guarantees with a whole lot of fine print, which often includes a promise *and* a myriad of exceptions to what is being promised. Neither Orkin nor Terminix ever offered their customers what Harvey came to refer to as a "no-nonsense" guarantee with a money-back feature.

"What do we have to do to make sure we can walk away from every imaginable encounter with every customer secure in the knowledge that the customer is satisfied with our service?" he asked. It was not a rhetorical question.

There was a lot of talk about following service policies and procedures, and about communicating clearly and directly so as not to create confusion between what the company had to offer and what the customer wanted, needed, and expected. There was discussion about reviewing the service agreement—it was never referred to as a "contract"—to ensure the customer understood what it said—or *promised*—and what it did not say.

"Can't we simply offer a guarantee to the customer?" someone asked. "Wouldn't that make it easier for the customer to trust us?"

Harvey's response was to remind everyone that no one currently doing business in the pest control, termite protection, or lawn care service industries offered anything resembling a guarantee.

"Why not?" someone else asked. "Just because it hasn't been done before doesn't mean it can't be done ever."

This interaction became an important teachable moment.

Harvey asked one of his managers to explain why there were no guarantees in the industry. Dave Armstrong, general manager at the company's flagship Clay Avenue service center at the time, explained that there were entirely too many situations—variables, he called them—over which the company had absolutely no control.

"Most houses have screens on windows," he said. "We aren't able to guarantee pests won't get into the house through a hole in a screen. Doors have bottom seals—or they're supposed to—specifically designed to keep bugs and other unwanted critters out, as well as to keep the house cool. We can't guarantee their integrity or that they're even there." He went on to talk about homes with crawl spaces, older homes with foundation cracks, and homes with children, who are constantly moving from inside to outside, opening but often not closing doors.

Dave accurately touched on just a few of the variables over which the company had no control and therefore couldn't or shouldn't accept the responsibility for guaranteeing. This led to a discussion of what would become known to some at Massey Services as the "infestation triangle."

"What are we really talking about here?" Harvey asked before answering his own question. "We're talking about the conditions, avenues, and sources of pest infestation." He drew a triangle on a white tablet atop an easel and wrote the words along the sides of it. "We're talking about the ways and means pests, who are creatures of the outside, get inside a customer's home."

Identifying the conditions, avenues, and sources of pest infestation would become an ongoing theme in customer communication and team member training moving forward.

"Why can't we turn what we already state in our sales presentation and what we include in our marketing materials into a guarantee?" someone asked.

Massey Services sales inspectors, especially when doing a presentation for Massey's pest prevention, always mention the company's commitment to customer satisfaction. This includes the stated promise that the service technician will come back to the customer's home as often as is necessary *at no additional charge to the customer* to remedy any situation the customer may be experiencing involving a pest infestation.

This brought the discussion back to the heart of the meeting: what could Massey Services do to make sure every customer was always satisfied?

One other issue had to be addressed first.

"What if we can't remedy the situation or satisfy the customer?" someone asked.

Harvey didn't miss a beat. "Then we give them their money back."

A moment of quiet came over the room. People looked at one another. Many of those in attendance were industry professionals at the service center and district management level, and at no time had anyone ever heard those seven words spoken out loud.

Todd Persons, from the company's agency, asked, "Can you

put this onto the service agreement? And would you be willing to say it in television and radio commercials?"

Again, Harvey didn't hesitate for even a moment. "Absolutely," he said, and just like that, the first money-back guarantee known in the history of the American structural pest control industry was born.

Massey Services Guarantee

Harvey closed out the meeting by reinforcing what everyone now understood would drive the company from that day onward. "If we don't have confidence in what we do, we shouldn't be doing it. If, for any reason, even an unreasonable reason, we can't remedy the customer's situation, they deserve their money back!"

• • •

The guarantee constituted a kind of touchstone for ensuring customers of Massey Services could be confident the company was able to do what it said it was going to do. This, in concert with the development of a few additional protocols for Massey's pest prevention service, led to a new marketing approach branded "A Partnership of Trust" between Massey Services and its customers.

Sales training began to include significant instruction in identifying those conditions, avenues, and sources of potential and actual pest infestation. This placed a portion of the responsibility on the customer to remedy those ways, means, and methods for how pests get inside the home in the first place that are beyond the scope of the company's service. Massey's role in the partnership of trust includes professionally administered applications of safe and effective products around the perimeter of the customer's property by a company-certified, professional service technician. This added a barrier through which most household pests would, theoretically, not gain access to entry.

"The guarantee isn't something we'll ever have to defend," Harvey said. "We were already providing it successfully. The only thing that changed was that we told renewing, new, and prospective customers we were offering it as part and parcel of our pest prevention service."

• • •

In the termite protection segment, it's fair to say such a revelatory guarantee was unnecessary because of the nature of the relationship between the customer and the company. When a customer bought termite protection from Massey Services, the promise was and is that if or when a customer experienced a new termite infestation and/or new damage, the costs associated with addressing both the infestation and the damage would be covered.

As far as the landscape services segment was concerned, a similar partnership of trust already existed. The customer agreed to leave the application of pest control and fertilization products to Massey Services. The customer's job was to properly mow, trim, edge, and water their lawn, trees, and shrubs, and they were provided with easy-to-understand information and instructions regarding exactly what those responsibilities entailed.

• • •

When all was said and done, the guarantees had as much—if not more—of a profound impact on Massey team members than the company's growing customer base. Internally, service technicians, lawn specialists, service managers, sales inspectors, and general managers all were able to project the confidence necessary to instill trust in the customers with whom they interacted. Watching the guy everyone referred to as the boss— the guy whose name was on the door—say out loud and on television that if a customer wasn't completely satisfied, they'd get their money back, created a sense of pride in the company, its methods, and in the roles they played in dispensing those services. And the knowledge that Massey Services was—for a while, anyway—the only company in the industry confident enough to offer such a guarantee was the whipped cream and cherry on top of the sundae.

• • •

The guarantee wasn't the only step Harvey Massey and Massey Services took in the early part of the 1990s to distance himself and the company from the huge pack of businesses, small and large, in the pest, termite, and lawn care industries.

Harvey liked to think about and talk about matters other than just revenue increases and profits. He spent time with people who understood such things, blue skying about the kind of business he wanted Massey Services to be. This later would evolve into the Massey Services brand.

He's always told anyone who will listen what's important to him, in order.

"Family, faith, vocation," he said, "are the foundational legs on which both I and Massey Services stand."

While his organizational structure was traditional and hierarchal, the way he practiced business was, as anyone who really knows him would attest, anything but.

"I've always believed that if you do the right things and if you do them right, and if you do them right and at the right time, all the rest takes care of itself."

"All the rest" included temporal matters such as revenue and profit. In fact, unless it was with his top tier of management and leadership, he seldom discussed anything related to those numbers. When addressing team members at any company function—be it training, visits to service centers, company events, or meetings—Harvey always talks about broader concepts, like doing the right things at the right time and doing them right.

Harvey Massey is a man of very strong faith, but unlike some others at his level, unless asked, he doesn't talk much about it. Instead, he lives it. He believes passionately about what he refers to as "walking the talk."

During the three-year period when he spent every August in Cambridge for Harvard Business School's Owner/President Management program, he learned that many global and national companies with leaders he respected had mission statements into which they enumerated their personal and corporate belief systems.

"I want everyone who works at Massey Services, or who does business with us as a customer or a vendor, to know who and what we are and what we believe," he said. "I want them to understand what we prioritize, how we think, and how we view the world, as well as our place in it."

These were ideas generally left to the giants, but one could be forgiven for not realizing what Harvey Massey envisioned about his company, even at a time when Massey Services was only a dozen service centers generating just under $10 million in revenues.

"Mostly," he said, "I'd like our team members to know and understand who they're in business with."

When asked what exactly he wanted to convey, he talks about the kind of words many business executives tend to shy away from. "We don't do a lot of strategic planning or major fine-tuning of any of our systems," Harvey said. "We operate our businesses every day, always making sure we're taking care of our people and our customers. That's job number one."

The Massey Services Mission Statement is comprised of a guiding philosophy, a statement of purpose, and a three-sentence mission statement. It hangs in every service center and is often a point of reference during daily meetings between service center general managers, service managers, and technicians or specialists. It touches on each of the elements Harvey Massey believes every team member and every customer needs to know about Massey Services.

"I worked on this for quite some time before I was ready to let anyone see it," Harvey said. "I always knew what I wanted to say. I just wanted to make sure when we put it before our team members, they would understand both the words themselves and exactly what they meant."

Massey Services was already living most of what Harvey incorporated into the Massey Services Mission Statement. Much of it constituted nothing new for the team members who'd been involved in the early stages of the company's growth. It simply hadn't been stated as formally and comprehensively as in the mission statement.

"There are some obvious stakeholders within our company," Harvey said. "Our customers and team members, for example. But we are a part of the communities where we do business. We're also part of an industry of professional operators and vendors. We all have families, friends, and associates in our lives and in our orbits."

• • •

It was Harvey's hope when the mission statement was completed and released that everyone Massey Services touched and everyone who touched the company would hold positive thoughts and experiences in their hearts and minds.

The mission statement, which remains today as it was when it was created, speaks to the company's customers and team members, to values such as truth and integrity, to image and to ongoing training, development, and education, to innovation and creativity, to community and industry, and to professionalism, all before it ever mentions anything about growth and profit. It addresses Harvey's and Massey Services' commitment to the protection of health, food, property, and the quality of our environment, and how the company strives never to be the biggest, but only the best company in its industry.

Another manifestation of the Harvey Massey way of thinking about things hangs in Massey's corporate office and in every one of the company's service centers. While most executives don't readily acknowledge the people who, for whatever reasons, choose to leave their companies, Massey Services wants team members to be able to say certain things about their experience when the time arrives for them to move on.

The poster reads:

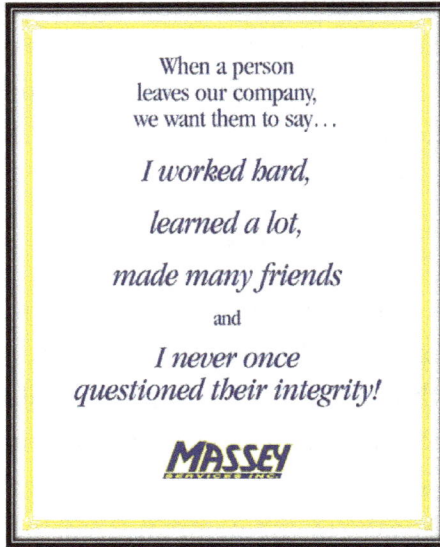

> When a person
> leaves our company,
> we want them to say…
>
> *I worked hard,*
>
> *learned a lot,*
>
> *made many friends*
>
> and
>
> *I never once*
> *questioned their integrity!*
>
> **MASSEY**
> SERVICES INC.

• • •

Both the guarantee and the mission statement have become part and parcel of the Massey organization's culture. They set a bar for how the company thinks about its valued relationships with customers, team members, and other stakeholder individuals and organizations.

The first plank in the mission statement links directly to the company's precedent-setting money-back guarantee. It reads, "Above all, we are committed to total customer satisfaction."

"It may be hard to imagine, but we don't really ever consider or worry about what our competitors are doing," Harvey said. "We measure ourselves against ourselves; we measure our performance against previous months, quarters, and years. We measure our customer growth as well as our customer retention and attrition."

In this regard, it's not unfair to consider the notion that Massey Services has no competition. In fact—and this will be addressed later in *When Your Name Is On the Door*—Harvey Massey has what might be a unique view regarding the other companies doing business in the pest management industry.

• • •

As this book is being put together, Massey Services is the fifth-largest company in the American structural pest management industry. It is the largest family-owned private company in the industry. While designations such as these would be sources of pride and inspiration for others, they don't resonate as much with Harvey Massey.

"I appreciate all that we've accomplished since February of 1985 when I purchased the Walker Chemical and Exterminating Company," he said. "We've managed to grow every single year through a combination of both internal expansion and cautious acquisition. But when someone asks me whether we'll ever 'catch' Terminix or Orkin, I typically smile and say something to the effect of, 'Well, we're not chasing them or anyone else.' If we're chasing anyone, we're chasing the very best possible version of Massey Services."

By instituting the very first customer satisfaction, money-back guarantee in the long history of the industry, and by publicly proclaiming the standards to which it holds itself as a company and as people, it's fair to say that the constant and unrelenting pursuit of excellence is the only "chase" of any importance to Harvey Massey and Massey Services.

Moments and Milestones

Chapter 5: 1997–2000

- Andrea Massey joins MPB Communications (1997) and graduates from Rollins College in Winter Park (1998).
- Angie and Shane Rignanese welcome their son Ryan (1997).
- Tony and Jann Massey welcome their son Colin (1998) and their son Bryan (2000).
- Jean Nowry joins the company (1998).
- John Milton joins the company (1999).
- Harvey Massey is named Professional of the Year by *PCT* magazine (1999) and is named one of the 25 Most Influential People in the Industry (2000).

Jean Nowry,
CFO

John Milton,
Regional VP

Massey Services – Internal Expansion, Acquisition 1997–2000

Expansion

1997
GreenUP, Lake County, FL

1998
Residential, North Villages, The Villages, FL
GreenUP Cocoa, Cocoa, FL
Residential, Tampa, FL
Residential, Marietta, GA
Residential, Fayetteville, GA

1999
Residential, Southeast Orlando, FL

2000
Residential, Clearwater, FL
GreenUP West Orange, Winter Garden, FL

Acquisition

1998
Marietta, GA

2000
Naples, FL

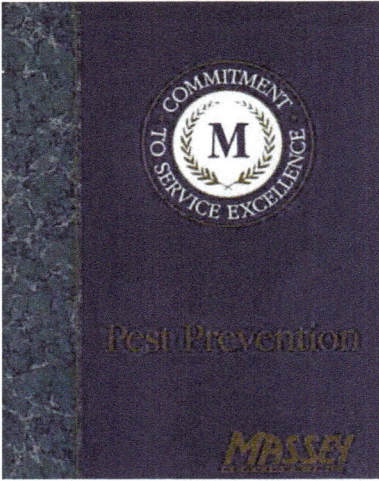

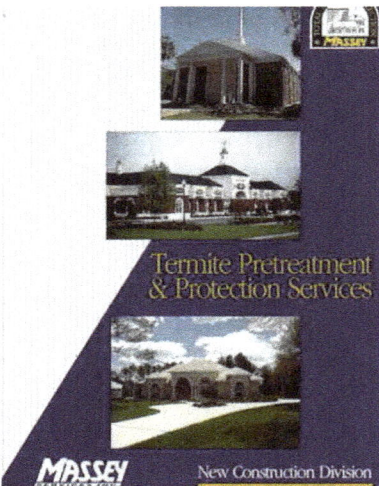

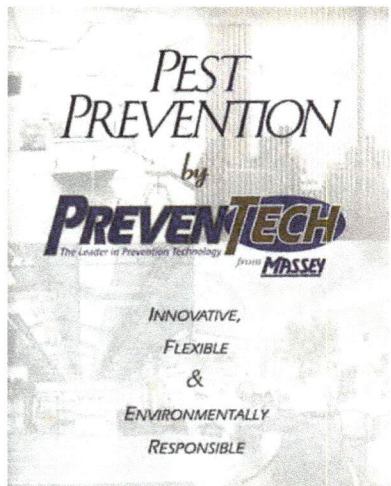

Massey service-specific sales folders

CHAPTER 6

Segmentation

"You can't manage what you don't know."

As Massey Services grew, Harvey Massey grew to understand the need to create a management structure that relied on segmentation of the company's business units.

"Even before we expanded outside of Central Florida, we were operating a number of distinct service businesses," he said. "While they obviously had characteristics in common, some of them also had individual attributes, including the method for delivery of the actual service and the type of customer involved."

Residential services include pest prevention; termite protection; and lawn, tree, and shrub care, including irrigation maintenance and repair and mosquito control, while the other two services—commercial pest prevention and new construction termite protection—deliver different types of services to different classifications of nonresidential customers.

"Our commercial customers require a different level of service," Harvey said, "and they often require that service beyond the scope of the typical business day. We provide pest pre-vention services to restaurants, hotels, health-care and skilled nursing facilities, commercial real estate buildings, large ware-houses, and manufacturing and distribution centers. In these situations, the customer often requires us to provide services after the end of the normal business day or even during over-night hours."

Some commercial businesses also required more than one service technician and specialized products and technologies. For example, traditional treatment for bedbugs often kept ho-tel rooms off the market for over a week. Massey's proprietary forced-air heat treatments returned hotel rooms to inventory in a matter of two days. The equipment required special tech-nician training, but the result was especially appealing to hotel operators.

There was, of course, crossover between residential pest prevention and termite protection customers and landscape services customers. Sales inspectors and technicians consistently cross-sold residential services, creating opportunities for cus-tomer discounts, as well as additional income for technicians.

"The customer might be the same, but the services them-selves are different," Harvey said. "The time necessary to perform services for individual customers often differs, as do the products used and the methods of delivery."

The new construction termite pretreatment business is a discrete service for a single customer type.

"In some locations—Florida, for example—every new home must be pretreated against infestation by subterranean termites," Harvey said. "Our customer in that case is the residential home builder, not the person or family moving into the house. This requires a different vehicle, differently trained technicians, and different treatment equipment and products, such as Sentricon bait stations and Bora-Care wood treatment."

All these offerings constitute individual segments and are provided to customers through distinct and discrete business units, but not necessarily from different service center locations. This is the essence of Massey Services' business segmentation model.

• • •

An interesting aspect of Massey's business is that most Massey service centers are seldom visited by customers. It's not that type of retail business.

"Ours is a service business, but unlike others—say, barbers or hair salons—we provide our service at the customer's home or place of business," Harvey said. "There's almost no reason for a customer to visit one of our service centers. It occurs on rare occasions, but very seldom."

Massey's business unit segmentation model is one of the reasons for the company's remarkable record of nearly thirty-seven consecutive years of incremental controlled growth in virtually every measurable metric, across all service types. Each distinct service has its own management structure and administrative function, as well as its own sales force and budget model.

There undoubtedly could have been some economies achieved by keeping some functions that cross individual segments together—administration, for example. Harvey Massey sees things differently.

"A stricter approach to segmentation allows us to focus more directly on each business unit in each market," he said. "You can't manage what you don't know. You can't adjust without knowing exactly how each segment in each marketplace is doing."

What might appear as an unnecessary expense becomes a more focused management tool on both the service center and business unit levels.

"Mostly, our service offerings are sold and marketed differently. The criteria for pricing are different in every instance. With pest prevention, it's a function of estimating the time a technician will need to professionally service the property. With landscape care, it's how much product and how much time will be required for how much square footage of lawn. Due to the individual geographic characteristics of a particular marketplace, it can make sense for us to operate two, three, or even all four business units out of a single physical facility," Harvey said. "It's rare, but not unheard of."

Not every Massey Services marketplace offers every service. This is the case for a variety of reasons. In some cases, acquisition of a particular business might generate enough of a customer base to establish a new service center for residential or commercial business. The individual nature of the marketplace, along with anticipated potential for growth, dictates when, which, or how many Massey service centers will be established.

Harvey subscribes to several of what he views as business truths. One of these, simply stated, is about managing the business every single day.

"Our segmentation approach is entirely a function of business management," Harvey said. "And you can't manage what you don't know. By breaking out individual service centers, even when they operate out of multiuse physical facilities, we can laser focus on all our internal budgeting and management processes. The more we know about how things are going in every facet of our business, the better we do."

• • •

As mentioned, Harvey Massey likes to remind his people of the words spoken by Professor Ben Shapiro of the Harvard Owner/President Management program: "There never was, is not now, and never will be a business model that is permanent."

This sentiment speaks volumes in the context of how Massey Services markets its services.

"Life was a lot simpler when I purchased the Walker Chemical and Exterminating Company back in 1985," he said with a chuckle. "Especially with regard to marketing."

The differences between how products and services were marketed back then, and the requirements of the marketplace today are—not to put too fine a point on it—staggering.

"Historically, most people thought of advertising as television and radio commercials, outdoor billboards, and print ads in newspapers and magazines," Harvey said. "But the advertising possibilities and the means of obtaining the customer's attention have evolved and fragmented dramatically over the years since we began our company."

In the early days, from 1985 through the early 2000s, Massey

Services relied entirely on traditional platforms—Yellow Pages, radio, television, outdoor, and direct mail—to place its name before potential customers.

"For a variety of already stated reasons, we invested heavily in Yellow Page directory advertising," Harvey said. "Usage of those cumbersome books is no longer how people find a service business when they decide they need one."

Yellow Page directories could be difficult to navigate. For example, if a homeowner wanted to protect his home from termite infestation and went to the listing for *Termite Protection*, in almost all cases, he'd be redirected to the *Pest Control* heading, where he might find literally hundreds of options from which to choose.

"In the BellSouth Orlando directory, during the early days, a customer could find more than a dozen and a half full-page ads, another dozen half- and three-quarter-page ads, and more smaller ads than he could ever get through," Harvey said. "Too many choices, all in one place, all at one time, all attempting to differentiate one company and one brand from another, can be daunting for the customer. Due to the way Yellow Page directory publishers do business, a new entry into a particular directory or category might have to purchase a full-page or even what's called a double-truck, or two-page ad, in order to quickly establish a competitive presence."

Still, for quite some time, a sizable segment of the potential customer marketplace relied on Yellow Page directory advertising to obtain residential services.

"Directory advertising was never intended to establish a

company's brand," Harvey said. "Television was much more effective at accomplishing that."

Need-based businesses—those that rely on a potential customer reacting to a real or perceived need—had fewer mechanisms for attracting new customers than those businesses aiming to satisfy a customer's wants.

• • •

Harvey Massey's approach to brand advertising eschewed humor, frivolity, and gimmickry. Instead, he wanted Massey's television advertising to teach both the consumer and Massey's team members.

"Advertising is expensive," he said. "I want to make sure we get as much bang for the buck as possible, and that includes making sure our messages are educational—at least to the extent we can actually do that in thirty seconds."

For the most part, television advertising is designed to imprint or brand a name or an idea into the memory of a viewer. It takes several impressions, or viewings, to accomplish that imprinting. This meant distilling the message, as much as possible, without losing the focus of the commercial. For purposes of illustration, one approach the company took in the 1990s turned out to be especially effective at both informing potential customers and educating Massey service technicians.

Over the years, Massey evolved in its television advertising. The company was not in the business of repurposing the messages of other operations. Instead, it had once again moved the entire industry with the introduction of a new, innovative service: pest prevention. This was more than just words; Massey's pest prevention constituted an entirely different approach to the existing pest control model, and the commercial needed to reorient the customer from the language of pest control to that of pest prevention.

"We didn't want to leave the image of spraying pesticides inside the home in the customer's mind," Harvey said. "There were, and are, times when that approach might be necessary, but we didn't want that to be the primary impression or message." Instead, Massey Services employed images not traditionally associated with pest control or prevention services.

"The word we used inside the company was *exclusionary*," he said. "The message was that pest *prevention* kept pests out in the first place, so they wouldn't have to be controlled later."

The images they used to make that message resonate included sealing spaces around cracks, crevices, and exterior water faucets, and caulking around doors and windows. The commercial also showed a particular home elevation under a protective covering, like a dome.

Another key to the success of this campaign was Harvey Massey speaking directly to the customer. He didn't speak into the camera; instead, he spoke to someone sitting out of the camera's view, an imagined customer, if you will.

"We were able to use the terms *conditions*, *avenues*, and *sources* in the commercial to reinforce the idea that not everything was necessarily our responsibility, but that we, our technician, would perform the exclusionary services after showing the pathways to the customer. It was that 'partnership of trust' approach between our customer and Massey Services."

An unseen announcer's voice set up and closed out the commercial revealed below in storyboard fashion.

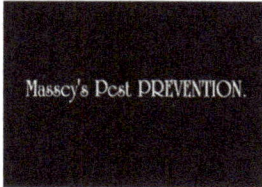

Announcer: *"Harvey Massey on the differences between pest control and Massey's Pest Prevention."*

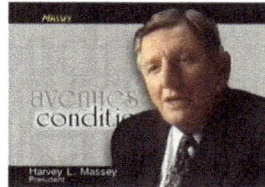

HLM: *"Massey's Pest Prevention eliminates the conditions, avenues, and sources of pest infestation.*

HLM: *"Things like sealing cracks and crevices,*

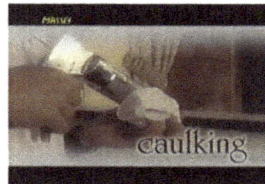

HLM: *"And caulking around windows and doors.*

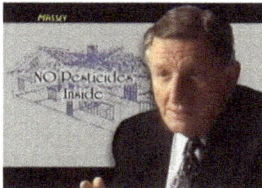

HLM: *"And that can mean no pesticides inside your home.*

HLM: *"If we keep pests out in the first place, we won't have to control them later.*

HLM: *"Someday, everyone will do it this way."*

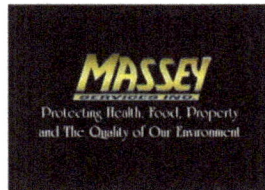

Announcer: *"Massey Services. Protecting health, food, property, and the quality of our environment."*

Massey Services Pest Prevention Television Commercial Story Board

Harvey's final spoken words, "Someday, everyone will do it this way," were designed to close viewers on the idea that pest prevention was revolutionary, and in so being, Massey Services was utilizing methods not employed by other operators. Once the announcer's voice and accompanying visual burned the company's tagline into the memory of viewers, the commercial was complete.

"It was impressive to me exactly how much could comfortably be included in a thirty-second television commercial," Harvey said. "This particular campaign was especially effective, in that our own people came to understand the important distinction between what we were doing and what everyone else was doing."

This aspect of what came to be known as "the Massey way" of doing things helped reinforce both trust and confidence inside Massey Services and outside in the marketplace.

• • •

Fast-forward to the middle of the first decade of the twenty-first century.

In 2007, new communication devices generically referred to as "smart technology" (phones, tablets, TVs, etc.) arrived in the hands and homes of America and the world. Smart technology connects people directly to the internet, to one another, and to a range of applications (apps) and platforms all designed to keep people and the world interconnected.

"The media landscape today is almost impossible to fully comprehend," Harvey said. "At least that's how it is for me."

Terrestrial (earthbound) radio has given way to satellite and streaming radio, with hundreds of channels and millions of subscribers. It is available in almost every vehicle and has been for years. Few satellite or streaming radio stations—Pandora is an exception—offer advertising opportunities.

Cable and satellite television is now available to almost every home in America. Subscription streaming services, such as Netflix and Amazon Prime, Disney+ and Apple TV have, for the most part, eliminated commercial messages during programming. Printed Yellow Page directories have all but vanished. Almost everyone can simply Google a business's name or type and obtain information instantly on their own.

This is why branding is more important and, at the same time, more elusive a concept than ever.

"People driving in cars may be listening to satellite radio, but they are still seeing outdoor advertising in the form of billboards," Harvey said. "People still receive direct mail solicitations delivered to their homes six days a week."

In the past, Massey Services predominantly marketed GreenUP Landscape Services via direct mail, door hangers, and brochures handed to customers by pest and termite technicians as opposed to television and radio. "We started out marketing to our existing residential pest prevention and termite protection customers and sent targeted mailings to potential customers who lived near homes we were already serving. They also got the reinforcement of seeing our spike signs in the lawns we serviced."

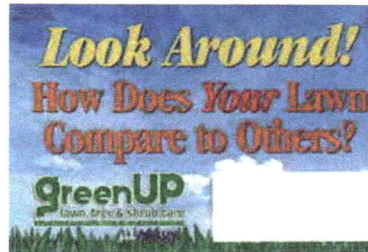

GreenUP Direct Mail Post Card

• • •

Massey's commercial services and new construction services are both sales driven as opposed to marketing driven. The people inside Massey Services responsible for growing these important segments understand that while most residential sales encounters are transactional, the arena is a bit more complicated in the commercial and termite pretreatment spaces.

"The commercial segments, including new construction, are based more on developing and then maintaining relationships," Harvey said. "We don't typically proactively market these segments with traditional advertising because the customers are already known to us and, most likely, we to them. The key is to be visible to them through their trade associations and membership activities. That way, lines of direct communication are kept open, and when their existing circumstances change, we're right there and ready to provide the services they require."

Of course, as with any business-to-business service organization, Massey's commercial and new construction sales representatives call directly on purchasing agents and departments.

"It's never advantageous to take for granted that anyone is simply going to call you," Harvey said. "We need to stay front and center with the people who have the responsibility for buying our services. In addition to having created, produced, and distributed branded sales material, we understood the need to be visible at their industry and association membership events, in their newsletters and magazines, and when possible, even sit on their boards of directors."

This type and level of activity is almost always directly connected to a service provider company's brand.

"As long as we remain true to our brand and keep our eyes focused on knowing the answers to three key questions, we'll be just fine. Those three questions are: who is our customer, where is our customer, and what does our customer want, need, and expect from us?"

When a service business knows the answers to these questions, it can transmit marketing messages both effectively and efficiently. And when a business honors its brand, all the rest typically takes care of itself.

Massey Services has invested significantly in branding Massey's pest prevention and termite protection as well as its GreenUP Landscape Services.

"By linking the Massey Services name with what we do, we give ourselves a bit of an edge in planting a response mechanism in the minds of consumers," Harvey said. "We still do things like that on television, the underlying theme being, 'When you need our kind of services, think of us.' But as with most businesses in the residential services sector, a strong and growing percentage of our leads today tend to come through our website and through internet browsers and search engines."

• • •

A business's brand is essential to its success. A brand is not a logo or an advertising tagline or some other physical mark or manifestation of its name. A company's brand is its promise to stakeholders.

"In our case," Harvey said, "it goes back to our guarantee and mission statement. It's our values. It's who we are. It's what we believe. It's the covenant between us and our stakeholders."

The services Massey provides to both its residential and commercial customers are grounded in the principles of trust and confidence. The relationship the company has with its team members involves integrity and truth.

"Whether someone comes to work at Massey Services or asks us to solve a residential or commercial service problem for them, we want them to intuitively accept as fact that they are involved with a company and people they can both trust and have confidence in," Harvey said. "It's foundational for us. We will always do what we say we are going to do."

And all signs point to the reality that Massey Services has been successful on all counts, in all its segments, with all its stakeholders.

Moments and Milestones

Chapter 6: 2001–2004

- Andrea Massey and James Farrell marry in Winter Park (2003).

Andrea Massey and James Farrell, 2003

- Angie and Shane welcome their son Jackson (2003).
- Tony and Jann welcome their son Aidan (2003).
- Tony Massey is named an Up and Comer by the *Orlando Business Journal* (2001).
- City of Orlando mayor Glenda Hood proclaims October 18 as Harvey L. Massey Day (2001).
- Massey Services receives the Environmental Excellence Award from the Orange County (Florida) Environmental Protection Division (2001).
- Eric Hernandez joins the company (2001).
- Adam Jones receives the Chipco Professional Products and *Lawn & Landscape* magazine Leadership Award (2002).
- The Jewish National Fund awards Harvey Massey its Tree of Life Award, and Junior Achievement of Central Florida presents him with its Spirit of Achievement Award (2002).
- The US Environmental Protection Agency awards Massey Services its first Pesticide Environmental Stewardship Award (2003) and its second (2004).
- Harvey Massey receives the Star of Gratitude Award from United Cerebral Palsy of Central Florida (2003).

- Ian Robinson, Jonathan Goetz, Lynne Frederick, and Adam Scheinberg join the company (2003).

(Top Row) Ian Robinson, VP of Business and Organizational Development, Jonathan Goetz, Regional VP, Lynne Frederick, SVP of Marketing (Bottom Row) Eric Hernandez, VP of Fleet and Assets, Adam Scheinberg, VP of Information Technology

- *PCT* magazine names Adam Jones one of the pest management industry's Forty Under Forty (2003).
- Harvey Massey receives the Rotary Club's Businessman of the Year (2004).

Massey Services – Internal Expansion and Acquisition 2001–2004

Expansion

2001
GreenUP Lake Mary, FL
Residential, Alpharetta, GA
Commercial Services, Ft. Myers, FL
GreenUP North Villages, The Villages, FL
Residential, Clermont, FL
Residential, Palm Coast, FL

2003
New Construction, The Villages, FL
Residential, N. Tallahassee, FL
Residential, Apopka, FL

2004
Residential, McDonough, GA
Residential, West Palm Beach, FL
Residential, S. Tallahassee, FL
Residential, Winter Haven, FL

Acquisition

2003
Tallahassee, FL

2004
Winter Haven, FL
Palm Beach, FL

Massey Services Corporate Headquarters, Groveland Street, Orlando, Florida

CHAPTER 7

Unstoppable Growth

"We were and are in a constant state of becoming."

The remarkable chart at the conclusion of this chapter reveals, with the exception of 2010, a consistent, thirty-six-year pattern of measured revenue and profit growth. This wasn't a happy accident, but a purposeful, step-by-step objective.

"There are really only two ways for a company such as ours to grow," said Harvey Massey. "We can do it through internal expansion or through acquisition."

For purposes of clarity, internal expansion is defined as organic growth flowing from within the company. Acquisition means buying an existing business from another operator and either adding to existing market penetration or establishing Massey Services in a new marketplace.

• • •

Internal Expansion

Even before the company's name was officially changed from Walker Chemical and Exterminating Company to Massey

Services, Inc., Harvey opened new service centers in Winter Garden, west of Orlando, and Port Orange, south of Daytona. Then, in 1987, just after the name change, he broke out the lawn care business in the Clay Avenue service center building. He also acquired a small business in Oldsmar, outside Tampa, Florida.

"It's important to remember," he said, "that we literally started growing as soon as the ink was dry on the purchase contract. Our company grew by 7 percent in 1985 and by 10.3 percent in 1986. We took an operation that had been stagnant for at least two years and breathed life into it."

From the very beginning of 1986 through the very end of 2021—a period of thirty-six uninterrupted years—Massey Services has seen consistent internal expansion and steady, conservative acquisition of business.

The year 2010 has been excepted from this construct because that was the year Massey Services acquired Middleton Lawn and Pest Control. The transaction was finalized on December 17, 2009, but the additional $50 million in revenue wasn't recorded on Massey's books until 2010. There is more devoted to that transaction later this chapter of *When Your Name Is On the Door.*

How does a business providing residential and commercial services in the fastest-growing environment in America grow via internal expansion in a controlled and measured fashion?

"From the beginning, we existed in a constant state of becoming," Harvey said, with a smile. "We were becoming better at what we do. We were becoming bigger, and more visible. We were becoming an important force in all our segments. We were becoming the company we were meant to be."

We don't want this book to become bogged down with statistics and numbers. That said, the chart referenced earlier at the end of this chapter reflects a growth pattern any kind of business—product-based or service-based—would be proud to present to the world.

"It was always important to me that we not lose control of the reins," Harvey said. "When I'm on horseback—something I've done almost my entire life—I never, *never* let go of the reins. I had to apply the same principle to keeping my attention focused on not losing control of the business."

Without bragging, Harvey recounted a story from his days at Orkin, when, as a thirty-two-year-old, newly minted vice president—the youngest in the company's history—he instituted some changes to how business was being done in Chicago.

"My experience with Orkin in Texas left me with the impression that our customers really wanted to do business locally. Some of these conditions don't come into play any longer because of smart technology and the internet, but when we started out, different towns, cities, counties, even neighborhoods had to pay a premium to call a single central number. Believe it or not, that inhibited opportunities for service businesses."

Once there was three-quarters or even half of a pest prevention route into a nearby community that required what Harvey viewed as too much time in the truck and not enough time in front of the customer, he and his leadership team would begin the process of identifying where to place a new service center to provide quicker access to those customers.

"We'd see if we could imagine enough potential for growth until it was time to place an ad in the Yellow Pages," he said. "This is how we did it in Chicago. We used direct mail in those zip codes, neighborhoods, and communities where we already had seen enough business to determine that the correct demographic conditions existed for expansion."

Using available research, including household income, home valuation, and numbers of addresses in proximity to the existing customers comprising that half or three-quarters of a Massey Services route, Harvey would employ direct mail, door hangers, and aggressive referral incentives to better penetrate a marketplace.

"It didn't take long before we'd have sufficient critical mass to make the investment and open a new service center," he said.

In the circumstances where there were already multiple service routes, breaking out a new service center meant the expansion center might achieve profitability almost immediately.

"By late 1991, we knew we needed to have a service center in Seminole County, Florida," Harvey said. "We already had business in what we called the North Orlando service center on Clay Avenue that could easily transition to being serviced from a location in Seminole County."

It didn't take long to identify Lake Mary as the prime location for this exercise in internal expansion.

"Another lesson learned from places like Chicago and Cleveland when I worked for Orkin involved how much time a technician would spend in his or her vehicle, especially during rush hour traffic," he said. "None of that was productive time, and it could, in the case of an accident or some other significant delay, push service back, even to another day, for a number of our customers. That wasn't something I wanted our people to have to deal with."

By moving two existing pest prevention routes from North

Orlando to Lake Mary, technician travel time was shortened, and revenues now attached to Lake Mary provided the impetus for additional, highly successful internal expansion in Central Florida.

• • •

Massey Services doesn't have a hard-and-fast template for a service center. There's no single model dictating physical configuration, how much space is needed, what security measures are required, etc. Instead, the company considers what it views as favorable terms for expansion.

"There's always commercial space available for either purchase or rent," Harvey said. "We need to locate in a safe environment for our team members, but we don't necessarily require what might be considered prime, main street, high-traffic frontage. That kind of space is more appropriate for a retail shop or a restaurant. It's also more expensive. Instead, we need secure space for our vehicles and our materials and supplies, sufficient square footage for our sales, service, and administrative team members and service functions, along with the right telephone prefix and zip code to create the impression for potential customers that we are a local or neighborhood business."

Finding the right physical location for an expansion service center became a question of how the expansion effort would work in both the "now" and the "then." Questions included lease flexibility, in terms of length and possible rental rate increases, as well as the possibility of physical expansion should the company decide to add a lawn care service center or a commercial services operation within the same physical facility.

"Since customers seldom visit our service centers, we could locate off the beaten path as long as team member safety and vehicle and product security conditions were met. We would always put a sign on our service center, but it didn't have to be physically located in a busy shopping area or on a high-traffic roadway."

Massey service centers come in all sizes and configurations. The primary drivers are, as with all real estate transactions, location and terms.

"Obviously, the first consideration for us had to be whether or not a particular space met our requirement that a technician's time in front of a customer take precedence over his or her time driving in a service vehicle to get to the customer," he said. "The next criteria or filter would be favorable lease terms. We prefer not to buy an existing building, and we don't build from the ground up to accommodate a service center."

An important aspect of any internal expansion effort requires Massey's ability to put people in place who are ready to accelerate the company's processes for obtaining sufficient customer density and revenue growth to justify and take advantage of the expansion opportunity.

"From the very beginning, we understood that people were the key to success with any kind of expansion," Harvey said. "We'd continually identify the technicians who'd be right for a service manager position and the service managers who could easily transition up into general management. Office managers were almost always promoted from larger service centers with existing administrative staff. With rare exception—acquisition, for example—almost all of our service center management positions are filled by promoting people already on our payroll."

• • •

Acquisition

In a manner of speaking, Massey Services began with an acquisition.

"Although the thought didn't occur to me at the time, I suppose we could have started from the ground up," Harvey Massey said. "But when the combination of ingredients presented by an established, fifty-five-year-old company in an ideal location and in almost perfect ownership and financial circumstances presented itself, it was as if it were preordained."

Harvey acquired the Walker Chemical and Exterminating Company in Orlando, Florida, from Stella and B.J. Walker on February 20, 1985, for $3.9 million. He usually puts it in the context of his life at the time. He'd just given up a top management job at what he'd helped grow into the largest company in the American structural pest control industry, Terminix. This followed a remarkable sixteen-year stint with Orkin, where he'd become the youngest vice president in the storied history of the company.

"I had it all," he said. "I was earning more than I'd ever imagined. I had the big corner office at Terminix corporate headquarters. I also had two children in college and one entering high school. It would be understandable to ask why someone in those circumstances would uproot his family, move to a new place, step into nearly four million dollars in debt, to purchase a stagnant business."

He harkens back to his favorite quote attributed to Mark Twain: "The two most important days in your life are the day you are born and the day you discover why you were born."

Harvey Massey was born to build this stagnant, fifty-five-year-old, $3.9 million pest control business into what it has become as of the end of 2021: a three hundred-plus million-dollar-a-year enterprise with over 170 service centers in nine states, more than 800,000 customers, and over 2,600 team members. As this book is published, Massey Services is the largest family-owned pest, termite, and lawn care business in America and one of the largest overall in the entire world

Harvey built Massey Services into the company it is through a consistent program of internal organic expansion and carefully executed acquisition. Since his first acquisition of Porter Pest Control in Orange Park, Florida, in 1988, Harvey Massey has acquired thirty-five additional companies with thirty-nine locations in Florida, Georgia, North and South Carolina, Louisiana, Texas, Oklahoma, and most recently, Virginia and Tennessee.

Pest Control Technology Magazine Industry Ranking Plaque

He's pragmatic regarding how this phenomenal process has unfolded over the years.

"Look, most of the larger companies in the industry have grown in this manner," Harvey said. "It's part of the nature of how this particular service business works."

The American pest management industry, as it exists in 2020, is made up of almost twenty-nine thousand small, mid-sized, and large businesses.

"The overwhelming majority of those businesses are relatively small operations generating under one million dollars a year in revenue. Most of the industry, which generates nearly eighteen billion dollars annually, is serviced by the top hundred or so companies."

Smaller companies account for most of Massey's acquisitions.

"The owners of many of those we've been able to acquire were typically older and ready to retire," he said. "In some cases, they simply no longer wanted the responsibilities associated with ownership."

It may surprise some, but Massey Services doesn't target businesses for acquisition or jump on every opportunity that comes its way. As this book is being finalized, Harvey Massey has been in the industry for over fifty-eight years. He's been on both the corporate and ownership side. He's worked with the giants and with relatively small operations. Over that time, he's made the acquaintance of hundreds of operators, most major vendors, several state and national trade groups, all the industry publications, and many allied individuals and businesses.

Many Massey Services leaders—President and recently named Chief Executive Officer Tony Massey, Chief Operating Officer Ed Dougherty, Chief Financial Officer Jean Nowry, Senior Vice President of Marketing Lynne Frederick, Senior Vice President of Customer Service Jeff Buhler, Vice President of Business Development Ian Robinson, and others—are actively involved in numerous industry organizations, events, and activities and are often approached regarding either merging or being acquired.

"We are constantly being made aware of possible acquisition candidates from people either connected with the company through a vendor relationship, someone directly interested in selling, or via the industry rumor and gossip mill," Harvey said. "We're at many state and almost every national meeting or convention. I think it can safely be said that a week doesn't go by without someone here being approached regarding us acquiring their business."

Despite the company's size and scope, even Massey Services itself is not immune to this dynamic of the American free enterprise system.

"We've been approached a number of times about selling Massey Services. It's always flattering, but ours is a family-owned-and-operated company, and, at least as far as I'm concerned, I think it's going to stay that way."

Not every company Massey looks at is a candidate for acquisition. While there is no template or formal checklist, several company leaders examine everything from the business's financials, image and reputation, employee retention, and pricing and compensation structures to its service processes, policies, and procedures. An early consideration always involves geography.

"I'm from the south," Harvey said. "We've lived almost entirely in southern states, except for a couple of years when I was with Orkin in the Midwest. The southern states are less susceptible to changes or differences in seasonality. While we wouldn't necessarily dismiss a possible acquisition out of hand because the company is not in the south, I think it's only fair and honest to point out that all of our acquisitions to date have been southern or southwestern businesses."

• • •

It was a big deal when Massey Services first expanded outside of Florida in May 1998. It wasn't very far outside of Florida, but it had a great deal of meaning to Harvey and within the pest management industry.

At the close of 1997, Massey Services had surpassed fifty-five thousand customers and was generating a bit under $22 million in revenues from thirty service centers in Florida.

"We were presented with a unique opportunity to move beyond Florida's northern state line," Harvey said.

Massey Services was contacted by an attorney for a Georgia operator. Harvey knew him from his days at Orkin. His client, RSA Services, had performed some termite work that was not 100 percent in compliance with state standards. Massey was asked to step in and bring the work up to state requirements. Following completion of the work, the same attorney made Harvey aware of an opportunity he couldn't ignore to purchase the company of another of the attorney's clients.

"The purchase of Environmental Pest and Termite in Marietta, Georgia, would become our largest acquisition to date," he said.

It would also be a harbinger of things to come.

Harvey Massey could not avoid industry speculation that by planting a flag in the Metro Atlanta marketplace, he was sending a signal to his former employer. It wasn't so.

"First of all, we didn't seek out this acquisition; it came to us," he said. "Second, we were little more than a flyspeck compared to Orkin. At the time, we were at twenty-two million dollars in annual revenue, while they were at nearly five hundred and forty million dollars. They are, today, the largest company in our industry and still among the most respected."

So, if it wasn't about showing up on Orkin's doorstep and announcing Massey's arrival in their home marketplace, why Atlanta?

"You have to remember, I lived in Atlanta twice while working at Orkin. I knew the area like I knew the back of my hand. Atlanta was then and still is today a powerful, vibrant, and rapidly growing marketplace brimming with opportunity. It would have been derelict of us not to look favorably at an opportunity to enter the Atlanta marketplace in 1998."

Derelict, indeed. Today, Massey Services, under the leadership of Regional Vice President Jonathan Goetz, has fifteen service centers generating over $19 million in Metro Atlanta, reaching nearly to Athens!

In addition, by the time *When Your Name Is On the Door* is published, Massey will have moved into Louisiana, Texas, Oklahoma, North Carolina, South Carolina, Tennessee, and Virginia through acquisition.

"The fact is," Harvey said, "we will hopefully continue to grow our business until we have a presence in Mississippi, Alabama, and Arkansas. It has never been our goal to be the largest company in our industry. That would require circumstances I can't even imagine. But as we say in our company's mission statement, we will grow, we will take care of our customers and our team members, and we will do everything within our power to be recognized as the best service company in America."

Clearly, Massey Services is well on its way to achieving that goal.

• • •

The Game Changer

Near the very end of 2009, Massey Services completed an acquisition that could be said to have been decades in the making.

"We were on track to complete our twenty-fourth year of growth in both revenue and operating profit, even though the nation had sunk into the deepest financial slump since the Great Depression of the 1930s."

By year's end, Massey Services would hit $78.5 million in revenues, albeit with just a 1.3 percent operating profit—the smallest in the company's history. Though all of that was about to change.

• • •

Harvey and Carol Massey counted Chuck and Lynn Steinmetz among their closest and longest-term friends until Lynn's passing in October 2012.

"We lived within walking distance of one another in Winter Park, Florida," Harvey said. "We traveled literally around the world together,

Charles "Chuck" Steinmetz and Lynn Steinmetz

spent countless hours in each other's company, and, I think Chuck would agree, despite being business competitors, never have had a cross word pass between us."

Harvey Massey and Chuck Steinmetz are both viewed as lions in the American structural pest management industry. Both have been highly successful in business. Both have been widely considered among the most philanthropic citizens—corporate and private—in the places where they've lived and done business. Both have supported education, health and human services, arts and cultural institutions and facilities. And, to this day, they are still the very best of friends.

They got to know one another while working with Rollins, Inc., parent of Orkin Exterminating Company. Chuck took the scientific path, having graduated from the University of Florida in Gainesville with a BS in entomology. Harvey rose in the business literally from the ground up by crawling under houses in Austin and San Antonio, Texas. In 1985, when Harvey bought the Walker Chemical and Exterminating Company in Orlando, one of the first calls he received was from Chuck Steinmetz.

"While I was at Terminix," Harvey said, "Chuck was building two companies: All- American Pest Control and Middleton." All-American would be rebranded under the Sears Termite and Pest Control umbrella and would ultimately be sold, first to Sears and then by Sears to Terminix. Middleton would continue under Chuck's leadership to grow into a large, multifaceted service organization remarkably similar and complementary in many ways to Massey Services.

Observers, as well as companies operating within the American pest management and landscape services industries, understand that there's a constancy of ownership movement. Companies are bought and sold all the time, due in no small part to the renewing revenue model, along with other attractive financial and operational aspects of these businesses.

"We get contacted regularly, even now, by both industry players and outside financial companies interested in buying our business," Harvey said. "As I've said, we have no interest in being anything other than a successful family business." Different operators have different aspirations.

In 2005, Sunair Electronics, through its wholly owned subsidiary Sunair Southeast Pest Holdings, purchased Middleton Lawn and Pest Control for an estimated $50 million in cash, stock, and a promissory note. At the time, Middleton was serving over sixty-eight thousand customers out of twenty-two service centers throughout Florida. At the same time, Massey was providing services to two hundred thousand customers from fifty-three service centers. They had expanded into Georgia and later that same year would move into Louisiana.

"After congratulating Chuck on completing the sale and joining Sunair's board, I had occasion to meet with Sunair's chairman, Richard Rochon," Harvey said. "After a cordial conversation, I casually mentioned that should he ever consider selling Sunair's pest, termite, and lawn care business, to please give me a call."

That call came approximately four years later.

"I know most companies and industries feel that their businesses are distinct among the vast plethora of organizations that make up the American economy," Harvey said. "Ours actually is, for a variety of reasons."

There are unique aspects to the residential services provided by organizations such as Massey Services and Middleton Lawn and Pest Control. Not the least of these involves the previously stated fact that service technicians and specialists are literally invited inside a customer's home.

"Sometimes—and I know this may be hard for some people to fathom—homeowners entrust our people with keys to their homes, as well as alarm codes," Harvey said. "This means we have to be extra vigilant in our hiring practices, which include stringent background, credit, and drug checks, along with our ongoing technician and specialist training regimens."

Companies in these spaces also regularly utilize products regulated by state environmental agencies, along with the federal government through the Environmental Protection Agency. While these aspects of doing business are second nature to operators like Harvey Massey and Chuck Steinmetz, organizations enamored with a business's financials often overlook these costly and complex operational nuances.

Sunair's chairman Richard Rochon asked his board member Chuck Steinmetz to reach out to Harvey and gauge his interest in buying Sunair's pest, termite, and lawn care business. The conversation was cordial and brief.

"From our standpoint, there really wasn't a whole lot to discuss," Harvey said. "We knew everything we needed to know in order to come up with an offer that was fair, as well as terms that were attractive." Plus—and this is important—the purchase coincided perfectly with one of Harvey Massey's and Massey Services' core cultural competencies.

"We have always, always believed that market penetration is a key to the effective and efficient delivery of services," Harvey said. "In so many instances, the customer base we acquired added route density. This meant less distance and travel time for our technicians and specialists, which translated into more time in the presence of our customer."

The cultures of the two companies—Middleton and Massey—meshed perfectly, thanks in great part to the close relationship that flowed between Harvey Massey and Chuck Steinmetz having grown up in the business together.

"During much of the time Chuck and I spent together over

the years, whether traveling or visiting at each other's homes, we discussed business. Granted, as competitors, we probably both held back on some things, but in general terms, we agreed on so much of the business fundamentals and on the values we both held so closely."

There also was some convenient cross-cultural pollination involving members of both companies' leadership teams. Lynne Frederick, Massey's current senior vice president of marketing, was in marketing at both All-American and Sears under Chuck Steinmetz. Jeff Buhler, who today is Massey's senior vice president of customer service, was Middleton's vice president of operations, and Ian Robinson, now Massey's vice president of business and organizational development, spent time at All-American and then Sears Termite and Pest Control as vice president of technical operations.

"So many of the Sunair/Middleton people on the administrative and on the operational levels benefited almost immediately when they joined Massey Services," Harvey said. "Most received incremental raises in pay and improvement in some benefits."

Massey Services' acquisition of Sunair/Middleton Lawn and Pest Control was officially completed in December 2009. In the first full year, Massey's revenues jumped 64 percent, from $78.5 million to just over $129 million. Operating profit nearly doubled. And the road was forever paved for Massey Services to rise to its status of fifth-largest company in the American structural pest management industry and the industry's largest privately held, family-owned-and-operated business.

The Middleton acquisition also began a decade of internal expansion and growth via acquisition that continues until today.

It would not be unreasonable to believe that Massey Services' future always was, is today, and promises to be extremely bright.

• • •

All expansion, whether through internal organic growth or acquisition, relies heavily on Massey Services' ability to place experienced, well-qualified people in service manager, general manager, and ultimately regional and divisional manager positions. Toward this end and not by accident, from day one, Harvey Massey placed a high priority on technical and leadership development at all levels of field and corporate operations.

"Almost no one comes to work for Massey Services with an established understanding of what we do and how we do it," Harvey said. "That's why an integral plank in our company's mission statement focuses on ongoing training and team member education for everyone interested in advancement."

Technical and leadership development falls under the purview of Jeff Buhler, Massey's senior vice president of customer service. Included in Jeff's portfolio are Massey's quality assurance department and Massey's learning and development functions, including Massey University and administrative trainers.

Jeff Buhler, SVP of Customer Service

"Jeff's team, as part of their responsibilities, maintains a constantly updated file of service manager, general manager, and other leadership position candidates to ensure our company has the strongest possible bench," Harvey said. "We have individuals focused on specific service segments—pest prevention, termite protection, lawn and land-scape care, as well as sales, office administration, and corporate administration—who conduct frequent sessions designed to help technicians, specialists, and other manager and leadership candidates achieve the knowledge base necessary to advance within our company."

Harvey believes—and thirty-seven years' experience bears out his beliefs—that advancement from within company ranks is essential for the long-term growth of Massey Services. "I experienced this dynamic of business myself. I worked my way up from residential service and sales at Orkin all the way to becoming, at thirty-two years of age, a regional vice president and then implemented a similar attitude and operation as senior vice president of operations at Terminix. Those mechanisms are still in place at those companies and will remain as part of our culture at Massey Services."

Moments and Milestones

Chapter 7: 2005–2008

- Andrea and James welcome their twin sons, Ethan and Edward "Tedy" (2005).
- Tony Massey is named one of Orlando's Forty Under Forty by the *Orlando Business Journal* (2005).
- The Central Florida Zoo opens the Massey Services Insect Zoo (2005).
- Marcelline (Marci) Baugh joins the company (2005).
- In September 2006, Tony Massey is named President and Chief Operating Officer of Massey Services.
- In July 2008, Massey Services relocates its corporate offices to 315 Groveland Street in Orlando.
- Harvey Massey is inducted into Junior Achievement's Hall of Fame and into the Pest Management Industry's Hall of Fame (2008).

Andrea and James with twins Ethan and Tedy

Marci Baugh, VP of Finance and Accounting

Massey Services – Internal Expansion, Acquisition 2005–2008

Expansion

2005
Residential, Gainesville, FL
Residential, Eustis, FL

2006
Residential, New Smyrna Beach, FL

2007
Residential, Vero Beach, FL
Residential, North Jacksonville, FL
GreenUP Clermont, Clermont, FL
Residential, Sarasota, FL
Residential, Brooksville, FL

2008
Commercial, South Orlando, FL
Residential, Lawrenceville, GA
GreenUP Jacksonville, Jacksonville, FL

Acquisition

2005
Baton Rouge, LA

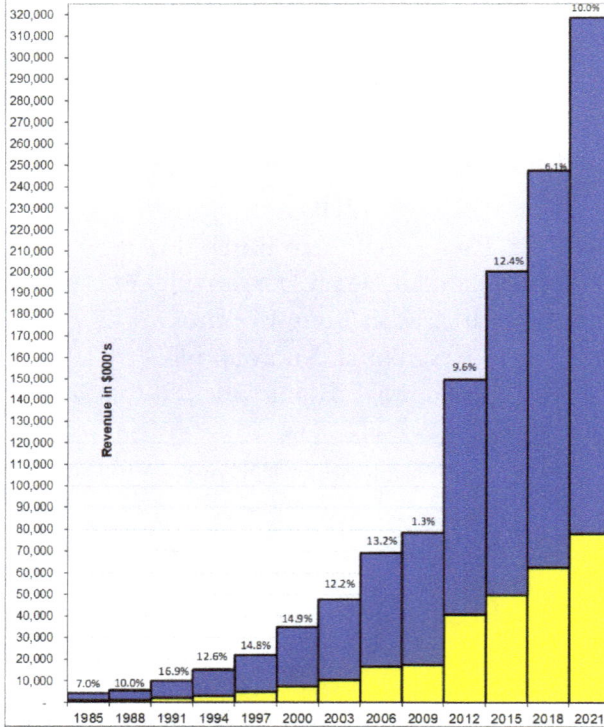

Massey Services, Inc.
Total Company Summary of
Gross Revenue & Service Center Profit
1985 - 2021

□ Op Profit ■ Rev

	1985	1988	1991	1994	1997	2000	2003	2006	2009	2012	2015	2018	2021
Total Rev	4243	5641	9953	15294	21852	34878	47660	69182	78536	149495	200200	247709	318379
Op Profit	874	1191	2315	3257	5098	7725	10518	16784	17477	40985	50000	62526	78327
Rev Incr %	7.0%	10.0%	16.9%	12.6%	14.8%	14.9%	12.2%	13.2%	1.3%	9.6%	12.4%	6.1%	10.0%
# of Service Centers	4	9	12	18	30	37	45	54	86	98	124	143	166

Massey Services Revenue/Profit Bar Graph, 1985-2021

THE FIVE BASIC FUNCTIONS OF MANAGEMENT

GROW Your Business
Sell!

SERVICE Your Customers
Quality & Quantity

COLLECT Your Money
"Cash" Pays Bills & Payroll

CONTROL Your Expenses
Make a Profit!

RECRUIT, Develop & Promote People
The Real Reward!

MASSEY
SERVICES INC.

CHAPTER 8

The Five Functions of Business

"The customer you have is as important, if not more important, than the one you're pursuing."

Growing up in Melville, Louisiana, Harvey Massey found himself immersed in small town life. This includes time spent with his maternal grandfather, Samuel Corte.

"One of my two enduring memories involving my grandfather was fishing for sac-a-lait, catfish, and brim fish in the Morganza Spillway," he said. The Morganza Spillway is part of a large-scale flood control system along the western bank of the lower Mississippi River. "The Atchafalaya River was too deep, too busy, and had a very strong current, so we fished, and occasionally even caught something, on the Spillway."

His other memory of time spent with his grandfather was working in the Corte General Store in downtown Melville.

"Melville wasn't very big," he recalled. "It was actually bigger back then than it is now, but my grandfather's store was pretty much the center of things in town. It ran for a whole block and sold clothing, fabric, hunting and fishing gear…pretty much everything. It was a classic, small town general store."

Harvey keeps a picture of Sam Corte in his office. It reveals the adult image of a proud, stoic Italian immigrant who arrived in the United States from Sicily at thirteen years of age in 1900.

Harvey's grandfather Sam Corte in the Corte General Store, Melville, Louisiana

"He showed up for work every day in a long-sleeved tan shirt, and always wearing a tie," Harvey said. "There was no air conditioning back then, and it could get very warm and humid in Melville, but he thought it was important for him to always look his best for his customers."

On Thursdays after school, Harvey would help his grandfather clean the store, and then the two of them would go fishing.

"We'd dust everything in sight, sweep the wood floor, and even water down the ground outside on the unpaved street," Harvey said. "Then, we'd tackle up and head for the Spillway. Sometimes, he and I would also go fishing again on Sundays, after church but before the entire family would assemble at his and my grandmother's home for Sunday dinner."

Harvey isn't certain whether or not the time spent with his grandfather talking, fishing, and working at the store informed some of his own future notions about business.

"I've been fortunate to learn something from everyone I've ever met and everything I've ever done," he said. "Some of my ideas about image probably date back to those early days with my grandfather—how he dressed every day in a shirt and tie, how he meticulously tended to the appearance of his store and its inventory."

Until Harvey began to rise within the vast hierarchy at Orkin, he didn't know all that much about how the service business worked. He credits Orkin for teaching him some important things about systems and procedures. Those basics—fundamentals, if you will—helped Harvey establish a simple yet powerful internal business structure for Massey Services.

"By the time I executed the purchase of Walker Chemical and Exterminating Company in Orlando," he said, "I'd come to understand, at least as it relates to what we do at Massey Services, what is required on a functional basis to operate a successful service business."

Over time, he distilled these key elements down to five specific fundamentals.

As part of Massey Services' culture, each service center, regardless of the segment in which it operates, is viewed by upper management as a freestanding business unit—an entity unto itself. In the general manager's office in each Massey service center, there's a poster proclaiming the Five Functions of Management. Company shorthand has reduced this to the "Five Functions."

The Five Functions are, in order, grow your business; take care of your customers; collect your money; control your expenses; and recruit, hire, develop, and promote your people. Harvey Massey teaches the simple idea that if a Massey Services general manager is not paying attention to these five functions of operating a business, they're likely focused on the wrong things.

"When a man or woman becomes a general manager with us," Harvey said, "they understand that they are effectively responsible for the operation of a business. They're not in business for or by themselves, but they are ultimately responsible for and are compensated based on the performance of their service center."

Massey's service centers each generate nearly $1.8 million a year on average. That's nearly $150,000 in gross revenue each month. Massey's operating profit hovers at around 25 percent. In some universes, this might be seen as pretty good. At Massey Services, this is considered baseline performance.

"The economics of our business are relatively simple to understand," Harvey said. "Everything, and I mean everything, relies on performance at the service center level. In truth, after our sales inspectors do their jobs, it all happens between the customer and the service technician or specialist. Everything else in our system supports and relies upon the service technician and specialist striving to meet the wants, needs, and expectations of our customers."

• • •

Grow the Business

Massey Services Sales Inspector

In Harvey Massey's world, if a business isn't growing, it's shrinking.

"There's no such thing as standing still in business," he said. "Incremental growth is the absolute essential and primary objective of any business, including, perhaps especially, ours."

At the residential service center level, a great deal of emphasis is placed on bringing aboard new mostly quarterly pest prevention customers, new annual termite protection renewals, and new bimonthly landscape services customers.

"The renewable revenue model is crucial to our success at Massey Services. That's why we view the customer we already have as at least as important, if not more so, than the customer we are pursuing."

One important method of growing the business is asking customers in one segment—pest prevention, termite protection, or landscape services—to purchase additional services. The cost per lead is next to nothing, and the cost per sale is minimal.

"We also regularly ask our existing satisfied customers to refer neighbors and friends," Harvey said. "We do this by having our technicians and specialists either ask directly for referrals or by handing or leaving them a referral request flyer or brochure."

The key to establishing a platform for sustained, ongoing growth is to ensure the highest possible rate of customer retention. That brings us to the second of the Five Functions.

• • •

Service Your Customers

Think back to the Massey Services Mission Statement. The first line in the guiding philosophy couldn't be clearer: "Above all, we are committed to total customer satisfaction."

Massey Termite Technician installs Sentricon Bait Station

"This is not a complicated concept," Harvey said, smiling. "We know what we're doing, and we know how to do it."

Massey Services is structured to include ongoing training and development of its frontline people to ensure its customers are in the best possible hands.

"Our service protocols are constantly updated so we can adapt to lessons learned in the field," Harvey said. "Originally, both our processes and our training focused on the industry model involving application of products inside the home to control infestation. When we evolved and developed our pest prevention platform, we changed the approach. The overwhelming majority of our work today happens outside, where pests live and breed."

In 1991, when Massey Services developed the first money-back guarantee in the industry, the bar was set especially high to make sure customers trusted Massey's promise.

"Again, it wasn't and isn't complicated," Harvey said. "We promise to return as often as necessary, at no charge to the customer, to solve any problem either flowing from or not previously addressed by our service."

Of course, on the extremely rare occasions when the problem isn't resolved, the company guarantees to refund the customer's last payment.

"Thankfully," Harvey said, "we don't have to do that very often."

• • •

Collect Payment for Your Services

This would appear as a given. Massey Services is, after all, a for-profit business in the clear spirit of the American free enterprise system.

"For the most part," Harvey said, "we don't have many issues with getting paid for providing our services."

At the outset of any relationship between Massey Services and its over 750,000 customers serviced from nearly 170 service centers in nine states, the customer is made aware of and agrees to in writing the terms of a formal service agreement.

"The overwhelming majority of our customers understand the importance of the services our company provides and pay for them either at the time of service or when they are invoiced. A significant number of our pest prevention and landscape services customers pay for services in advance and take advantage of a prepayment discount for doing so."

On the extremely rare occasions when there is an issue, everyone from the technician or specialist all the way up the line to service center management and even corporate leadership is empowered to work with the customer to reach a satisfactory resolution.

"We take a certain amount of pride in the fact that we don't litigate with customers," Harvey said. "The nature and structure of our customer demographics, our service offerings, and our approach to doing business is designed to prevent this from becoming an issue."

• • •

Control Your Expenses

If there is one of the Five Functions that requires the most management attention and oversight, it's controlling expenses.

"I've learned over the years that people often don't think about controlling expenses until it either surfaces as an issue or it's one of the metrics upon which they're evaluated," Harvey said. "It's also something we can't always objectively forecast during the budgeting process."

Typically, the largest single expense in a service center after staffing involves vehicles. There's operating expense, vehicle maintenance, and vehicle replacement costs.

"Maintenance and replacement are manageable and can be budgeted every trimester," Harvey said. "Where we get to make up ground is when we can reduce travel time for technicians and specialists and increase time in the presence of customers."

The potential of a Massey Services service center can either be enhanced or sabotaged depending on the manager's ability to control expenses. After focusing sales efforts on neighborhoods already filled with Massey customers, retaining customers through delivery of outstanding service and then asking satisfied customers for referrals, keeping receivables in check, and controlling expenses wherever possible, the only function that might inhibit Massey's growth potential would be not having a bench of frontline service management and general management candidates.

• • •

Recruit, Hire, Develop, and Promote Your People

Harvey Massey Conducts Training Session

There are few, if any, barriers to a team member's ability to move up within Massey Services. Regional managers' and vice presidents' job descriptions include developing candidates to move into existing and future management positions.

"There's a facet of being a working American that programs him or her to seek the highest possible standing," Harvey said. "It's called ambition. Those who have the drive but can't do it where they are will seek opportunities elsewhere. Our job as managers and leaders is to make sure everyone who wants to move up in our company, and who is qualified to move up, has that opportunity."

There is never a time when Massey Services isn't recruiting and interviewing for service technicians, landscape specialists, sales inspectors, and office administrators. The company may not be hiring for a specific position at a specific service center, but there are always opportunities to join the Massey Services team, because outstanding people are always being promoted.

"We've learned through experience that there are going to be people who want to move up within our company," Harvey said. "There are also people who reach a certain level and are satisfied to remain in those positions. And, of course, there are others who, for a variety of reasons, make the decision to move on. We value everyone who wears the uniform, works in the service center or in the corporate offices."

Because of the nature of the business, which involves technicians and specialists working around and sometimes inside a customer's home or business, Massey Services conducts stringent background and credit checks on every applicant being considered for employment. There's comprehensive testing, including drug screening, and multilevel interviewing for every position. Massey Services offers highly competitive compensation arrangements, including the ability to earn bonuses. The company also offers excellent, wide-ranging team member benefits and an award-winning, company-matched 401(k) program.

"Massey Services is often cited as one of the best places to work in the marketplaces where our company does business," Harvey said. "We have people who've been with us since the company was established in 1985, and we have new team members joining virtually every week. We take pride in the certainty that Massey Services is a great company for anyone seeking the opportunity to launch a successful and rewarding career."

On the business operations level, Massey Services conducts comprehensive budgeting sessions three times each year.

"Trimester budgeting is one of the most important management exercises in which we engage," Harvey said. "I hear our people say it's both exhausting and invigorating. In our case, it is a management tool essential to our company's success."

Even as Massey Services has grown from a $3.9 million company to a giant in the American pest management industry, bringing in over $300 million in revenue annually, every business unit that bears the Massey name submits an aggressive operating budget for management approval every four months.

"In April, August, and December, every general manager (GM) submits a budget detailing both revenues and expenses designed to provide a template for profitably growing his or her business," Harvey said. "After regional managers and vice presidents complete the process with the service center GMs under their leadership, they present budgets for their regions and divisions up the line, until EVP and COO Ed Dougherty signs off on leadership's expectations for the next four months."

Performance against previous budgets allows senior executives at Massey Services to gain a clear understanding of where their focus needs to be.

"It's like we said earlier," Harvey Massey said. "You can't manage what you don't know."

The trimester budgeting sessions examine the plan each service center general manager agrees will form the basis for his or her evaluation. They also provide the baseline for the next trimester, in terms of revenue growth and operating profit.

"Each service center provides a projection of revenues from sales of new business, as well as payment for recurring pest prevention, termite renewal, and landscape services revenues," Harvey said. "This is then weighed against anticipated expenses for each service center's vehicle-related costs, materials, and supplies, team member compensation and benefits, facility rentals, etc."

A careful examination by experienced regional managers and vice presidents focuses on where additional management is required and where opportunities for profitable growth exist.

"This is exactly why we perform this exercise," Harvey said. "Some businesses like to take a single look each year without any review along the way. We decided early on that in a service business like ours, more focus more often is an excellent way to adjust—fine-tune, if you will—as often as is necessary to keep everyone on his or her toes. I think our year-over-year revenue and operating profit performance is testimony to the efficacy of that process."

• • •

Harvey Massey likes to say that there are exactly 100 pennies in every dollar, not 95 and not 105.

"There are only a couple of rules in our budgeting process," he said. "First, we never budget to lose money. Even during difficult times, as was the case during the recession in 2008 and 2009, through belt-tightening and a laser focus on potential difficulties and opportunities, we've been able to keep team members employed, and we were able to grow and operate profitably."

The second rule has to do with those hundred pennies.

"We know where the majority of expenses are going to be," he said. "The variable is on the revenue side. In other words, we back into what we need from sales, payment for existing services, and termite renewals to cover expenses and to establish a profit target of at least 25 percent."

• • •

The Five Functions are: grow your business, service your customers, collect your money, control your expenses, and develop your people. This formula, in concert with budgeting every four months to operate profitably, is the cement between the bricks in the foundation of every single business unit operating under the umbrella known as Massey Services.

Moments and Milestones

Chapter 8: 2009–2012

- Angie and Shane Rignanese's daughter Kallie graduates from John Paul II High School in Tallahassee (2011).

Kallie Rignanese, Harvey and Carol Massey

- In 2009, Harvey Massey receives the James B. Greene Award from the Metro Orlando Economic Development Commission and the Richard L. McLaughlin Volunteer of the Year Award for the East Central Florida Division of the Florida Economic Development Commission.

- Jewish Family Services awards Harvey Massey the George Wolly Community Leadership Award (2009).

- He receives the Florida Citrus Sports' Howard Palmer Award (2010).

- Ed Dougherty is named Executive Vice President of Operations (2010).

- Andrea Massey-Farrell is named a Woman of Distinction by the Girl Scouts Council of West Central Florida (2011).

- Adam Scheinberg is named one of the Forty Under Forty by the *Orlando Business Journal* (2011).

- *PCT* magazine and Syngenta name Tony Massey a Crown Leadership Award winner.

- Andrea Massey-Farrell is one of the *Orlando Business Journal*'s Women to Watch (2012).

- Harvey Massey receives the Ernst & Young Entrepreneur of the Year Award and the ACG Smart Award (2012).

Massey Services – Internal Expansion, Acquisition 2009–2012

Expansion

2009

Residential, Central Villages, The Villages, FL
GreenUP Central Villages, The Villages, FL
Residential, Pensacola, FL
Residential, Bradenton, FL

2010

GreenUP West Palm Beach, West Palm Beach, FL
GreenUP Brooksville, Brooksville, FL
Residential, St. Augustine, FL
GreenUP Oldsmar, Oldsmar, FL
GreenUP Tampa, Tampa, FL
GreenUP Lakeland, Lakeland, FL
GreenUP Clearwater, Clearwater, FL
GreenUP New Smyrna Beach, New Smyrna Beach, FL
GreenUP Deland, Deland, FL
Residential, Palm Coast, FL
Residential, Lakeland, FL
GreenUP Naples, Naples, FL
GreenUP Melbourne, Melbourne, FL
GreenUP Sarasota, Sarasota, FL

2011

GreenUP Eustis, Eustis, FL
Residential, Avalon Park, Orlando, FL
Residential, Lake Nona, Orlando, FL
Residential, Longwood, FL
Residential, Windermere, FL
GreenUP Ormond Beach, Ormond Beach, FL
GreenUP Apopka, Apopka, FL
GreenUP Lake Nona, Orlando, FL

GreenUP Longwood, Longwood, FL
New Construction, Tampa, FL
Residential, New Tampa, Tampa, FL
GreenUP New Tampa, Tampa, FL
Residential, Port Charlotte, FL

2012

GreenUP Vero, Vero Beach, FL
Residential, Euless, TX
Commercial, Dallas, TX
Commercial, Houston, TX
Commercial, San Antonio, TX
Residential, Dallas, TX
Residential, Jacksonville Beach, FL

ACQUISITION

2009

Tallahassee, FL
Middleton Lawn and Pest Control, Orlando, FL

2012

Dallas, TX
Jacksonville, FL

MASSEY
SERVICES INC.

"A Company Above the Rest"

Massey Services is a leader in providing an environmentally responsible and superior service.
We adhere to the highest standards of performance and professionalism and continually
endeavor to be recognized as the best service company in the industry.

Ethics & Values

- The FIRST recipient of the 2005 Public Relations Society of America's Frank R. Stansberry Ethics Award for fostering a culture of ethical behavior towards Customers, Vendors and Team Members.

- The ONLY Company in Florida certified to teach termite protection to the building industry for Continuing Education Units.

Environmentally Responsible

- A CHARTER MEMBER of the U.S. Environmental Protection Agency's *Pesticide Environmental Stewardship Program (PESP)*.

- TWO-TIME RECIPIENT of the U.S. Environmental Protection Agency's *Pesticide Environmental Stewardship Program (PESP) Champion*.

- RECIPIENT of the Orlando/Orange County Environmental Excellence Award.

- The ONLY Central Florida Company in the industry to be asked to sponsor Earth Day.

Innovation

- The ONLY Company in the industry recognized by *Pest Control Technology Magazine* as the prototypical service company for the new millennium.

- The Company that CREATED the environmentally responsible approach of ***Pest Prevention*** instead of the spraying techniques associated with traditional pest control methods.

- The company that CREATED ***TOTAL COVERAGE Termite Protection*** - protection against all kinds of wood destroying insects.

- Recognized as ONE OF THE TOP ***Lawn Care Companies*** in America by *Lawn & Landscape Magazine*.

- One of the FIRST regional companies in our industry to receive the QualityPro Mark of Excellence in pest management by the National Pest Management Association.

Image

- The ONLY Company in the industry to be named *"**Best Dressed**"* by the American Uniform Association.

Expect More ...And Get It!
1-888-2MASSEY ◆ www.masseyservices.com

PA061

02/07

CHAPTER 9

Image and Reputation

"If you don't get the look right, you'll never get the act right."

Harvey Massey learned many valuable and enduring lessons while he served in the US Army Security Agency and during his twenty-two-year career with Orkin and Terminix. At least a couple of these lessons have served him and Massey Services well over the ensuing three and a half decades following his purchase of the Walker Chemical and Exterminating Company in February 1985.

The first has to do with the whole idea of a uniformed service and the subliminal discipline it instills and represents. The second involves the importance of image and reputation as they relate to a company's brand. Any conversation involving image and reputation must begin with the Massey Services Mission Statement.

"We have many constituencies," Harvey said. "It doesn't matter if we're talking about our customers, our team members, the communities where we do business, or the industry in which we operate. Every one of them is impacted by the image we project and the reputation we enjoy. And we address all of them in our company's mission statement."

Harvey has been conscious of the importance of these attributes for all his adult life.

"I was nineteen years old when I enlisted in the US Army and was assigned to the Army Security Agency," Harvey recalled. "I saw myself basically as an average young man at that age, and, as it did with many others, my time in the service left an indelible impression."

After he left the army, followed his heart to Austin, Texas, and went to work at Orkin, he was reminded of the value of discipline and uniformity in pursuit of goals and objectives.

"I knew if I took my training seriously," he said, "respected those in authority, and followed Orkin's prescribed policies and procedures, I stood a good chance of being successful. I had a young wife and a baby girl born two and a half months premature. Those were powerfully motivating responsibilities for me. I didn't even consider failure to be a viable option."

As has been covered in *When Your Name Is On the Door*, during Harvey's time with Orkin, then Terminix, and for the past thirty-seven years at the helm of Massey Services, there hasn't been a single moment even closely resembling failure.

• • •

Image

The US Army's basic training program is centered around ideas of discipline—following orders and procedures, respecting superior officers— and uniformity. It's not a place for individualism or outside-the-box thinking. Those attributes come later, when soldiers have already proven themselves ready to assume responsibility for and authority over others. The field operations people at Orkin, Terminix, and Massey Services experience something similar. Just as with the US Army, working in residential and commercial services requires discipline, adherence to policies and procedures, and uniformity, especially when dispensing services.

"From the very beginning, it became clear to me that we had to hire and train people who were interested first in learning about us—what we do and how we do things—and then indicated a desire to pursue a career with us," Harvey said. "At Orkin, after proving myself capable of learning and then performing a well-established program of both sales and service techniques, I was able to teach others how to execute Orkin's program of sales and service policies and procedures."

But simply wearing a uniform and following orders wouldn't be sufficient for people like Harvey Massey. With a clearly defined mission to build Massey Services into the best service company in the industry, he made it a standard practice to recruit, hire, develop, and promote a specific type of "soldier."

"As anyone who has served in any branch of the American military would tell you, there are those who follow orders and do their jobs, and then there are those relative few who also follow orders and do their jobs but stand out from the pack. Those standout performers are the people we target to recruit, hire, and develop and who today provide most of the leadership in our company."

One of the most important attributes of those standout performers is a commitment to projecting an outstanding image.

"It's surprising," Harvey said, "how many people in business settle for average or mediocre in the people who interact with their customers. Average and mediocre may be fine for some, but that's not going to cut it for very long at Massey Services."

People who wear the Massey Services uniform and demonstrate a desire to be successful and rise through the ranks into management and leadership follow a very simple creed: to be successful, you must look, act, and feel successful.

"If you never get the look right," Harvey said, smiling, "you never get the act right. It all begins with looking sharp, from first thing in the morning until you're finished for the day."

Looking sharp at Massey Services includes not just wearing the uniform, but wearing it proudly and making sure it's crisp, clean, and buttoned up. It includes clean hands, clean fingernails, proper grooming, fresh breath, and a smile. It includes, "Yes, sir," "No, ma'am," "Please," and "Thank you."

Since every Massey team member who finds themselves in the presence of a customer is typically driving a white service vehicle emblazoned with the Massey Services logo, the vehicle must also reflect these ideas of a proper, first-class image.

Multiple award-winning service technician Danielle Whitley

"Everyone who drives a company vehicle is responsible for the proper appearance, cleanliness, and maintenance of that vehicle," Harvey said. "Every team member at our company understands that when you wear the uniform, drive the vehicle, provide the service—any time you're in the presence of a customer or a prospective customer—you *are* Massey Services."

Harvey would be the first to admit that this is not an easy

standard to set or to live up to, but as the title of this book represents, when it's your name on the door, these are the kinds of things that separate a run-of-the-mill ordinary business from an outstanding service organization.

• • •

Projecting a first-class image begins with the team members who find themselves interacting with both customers and prospective customers. It extends to everything bearing the Massey name, from company vehicles, marketing materials, and television and digital advertising to signage at service centers and corporate facilities, as well as the entire Massey Services corporate staff.

"It really doesn't matter what manifestation of our presentation to the public we're talking about," Harvey said. "All people, including us, find ourselves, at times, in the role of customer. This means we make instant judgments about the people and, by extension, the companies with whom we're considering doing business. The phrase may be a bit overused, but you never get more than one chance to make a great first impression."

The same expectations regarding image imposed on team members who sell and provide services directly to Massey's customers apply to service managers and general managers at all Massey service centers, regional and divisional managers and vice presidents, all the way up to the executives who support the company's field operations at Massey's expansive corporate facility in Orlando, Florida.

"Most days, everyone at the corporate office dresses in business attire," Harvey said. "We can't expect our team members in the field who come here for whatever reason to see us in any way other than at our very best."

Similarly, all of Massey's marketing materials are proofed

The Massey Services Corporate Information Technology Group

prior to production to eliminate even the slightest possibility of a mis-spelling or misuse of language. The images depicting people, vehicles, equipment, or products are care-fully crafted and staged to leave no errant impressions with consumers or prospects.

Some might wonder why so much attention is paid to some-thing as open to interpretation as image in the pest prevention, termite protection, and landscape services business. This sug-gestion elicits a smile from Harvey Massey.

"As with so much of this, there's nothing really complicated about it. If you're in the presence of a customer, for anything, any product or service, you want to make as good a first im-pression as you can. Well, we're all customers for something. We don't want to see the people or companies with whom we're doing business looking or behaving any way but their very best. It's a statement about who you are."

It may not be complicated, but it's not easy, and it's never taken at all lightly by anyone at Massey Services.

"Why would we not aspire to provide the same kind of presentation to the people with whom we wish to do business as we would expect from a person or company who wants to do business with us? We wouldn't. And we don't."

• • •

Reputation

If a person's or a company's image is what is projected by that person or company to their customers or other constituencies, their reputation is a result of having lived up to (or in the negative, having failed to live up to) the image they've projected. Said differently, image is how you present yourself to others; reputation is how you are perceived and spoken of.

"We tell anyone who will listen that our first priority, as outlined in our now thirty-year-old mission statement, is 'Above all, we are committed to total customer satisfaction,'" Harvey said. "Everything we do is in pursuit of that commitment."

Saying the words is easy. Fulfillment of those promises isn't.

"We know, inherently, that we are not going to be able to satisfy every single customer every single time," Harvey said. "That stated, we also know that we're going to do everything we possibly can in pursuit of just that. It's essential for everyone to understand that this line of thinking is at the core of our system of beliefs. It's who we are."

• • •

Massey Services is, by most methods of measurement, a very successful company. It is, at publication of this book, well into its thirty-seventh year of uninterrupted growth, even including the years of the American recession in 2008 and 2009, as well as the time of COVID-19 from early 2020 through publication of this book. In a residential and commercial services company, this is an unassailable record of achievement. It points to two important metrics.

"First, we're extremely proud of our record when it comes to retaining our customers," Harvey said. "Second, we're equally, if not more gratified regarding our team member retention numbers."

It's easier for a company to grow when it keeps its existing customers satisfied, and it's also infinitely easier for that company to keep its customers satisfied when its experienced, professional team members stay with the company. Such is the case with Massey Services.

It could be suggested that satisfied customers and satisfied team members are the two most important indicators of a company's reputation. There are, however, some other metrics specific to Massey Services that contribute to its stellar reputation among virtually all constituent groups, even its competitors.

"With very few exceptions, we don't litigate with our customers. There's this bromide in business that the customer is always right. We put it slightly differently. The customer may not always be right, but the customer is always the customer. And our commitment is to his or her total satisfaction with our services."

Experience has taught Harvey that satisfied customers tend to tell a handful of neighbors and friends how happy they are with a company's service or product. Unhappy customers tend to tell *everyone* they meet of their dissatisfaction.

"You have to *always* make the effort," he said. "The customer you have has the potential to purchase another of your services. They can refer you, proactively, to friends and neighbors. This makes growing the business much easier than if your newly acquired customers are simply replacing dissatisfied ones who have left."

• • •

A company tries, either consciously or otherwise, to create a connection between their brand and certain thoughts and feelings. When someone hears the name Massey Services, Harvey wants them to recognize the name and know exactly what the company does.

"It's important—no, it's essential—that we plant certain notions and ideas about Massey Services in the hearts and minds of our team members, as well as both current and future customers," he said. "For example, we want them to know, intuitively, that they can trust us to be able to do what we say we're going to do. We also want them to have the confidence in us that we will do what we say we're going to do. Those are two different ideas."

As discussed in Chapter 5 of *When Your Name Is On the Door*, these two attributes, trust, and confidence, are cornerstones of Massey's brand and promise to team members and existing and future customers.

"We want our reputation to reflect the image of professionalism, politeness, and confidence projected by our people," he said. "We also want it to answer, in advance, any questions the customer might have regarding our commitment to their total satisfaction."

• • •

Through company leadership activities, which will be discussed in the next chapter of *When Your Name Is On the Door*, Massey Services builds and maintains a connection between its brand and its customers, team members, the industry, communities where it does business, and a commitment to the protection of our environment.

"Some people suggest that a company like ours, in the pest prevention, termite protection, and landscape services segments, can't refer to itself as environmentally responsible," Harvey said. "What we've discovered over the past thirty-seven years is that what we do and, more importantly, how we do it, is unequivocally consistent with the core principles of environmental stewardship."

After dropping the Walker Chemical and Exterminating Company name, Massey Services quickly established itself as an industry leader in the safe, effective, and responsible use of pest prevention, termite protection, and landscape services products. For example, Massey's residential pest prevention program focuses its services and application of products outside the home, where pests live and breed, as opposed to spraying pesticides on baseboards and into cabinets inside the home.

Massey reduced soil saturation perimeter termiticide treatments in favor of Sentricon baiting and Bora-Care wood treatment, which saves significantly on the use of water and, specifically in the case of subterranean termite protection services, on the use of products that could potentially contaminate groundwater.

Massey's landscape services program focuses on educating customers about proper watering and mowing techniques while utilizing granular fertilizers as opposed to liquids, which could leech into lakes, streams, and groundwater.

Put together, all these practices have been introduced by responsible operators throughout the industry, thanks to Massey Services' leadership.

"Like so much of what we've been talking about, it really all goes back to our mission statement and the fact that every one of us strives to live it every day. It's called 'walking the talk,' and we know we're going to have to work harder and more diligently to make sure that our brand always reflects its beliefs and core values," Harvey said.

For thirty-seven years, Massey Services has set the standard in all its industry segments for presenting a positive image of the American pest prevention, termite protection, and landscape services marketplace. Under the leadership of Harvey Massey and President and CEO Tony Massey, the largest family-owned-and-operated company in our nation's structural pest management industry enjoys an unmatched reputation for professionalism, innovation, industry and community leadership, and environmental stewardship.

Moments and Milestones

Chapter 9: 2013–2016

- Kallie Rignanese graduates from Florida State University in 2015 with a BS in sociology.
- Ryan Rignanese graduates from FSU High School in 2015.
- Gwyn Elias is promoted to Chief Investment Officer, Jean Nowry is promoted to Chief Financial Officer, and Eric Hernandez is promoted to Vice President of Fleet and Assets (2014).
- Harvey and Carol Massey establish the Harvey and Carol Massey Foundation and install Andrea Massey-Farrell as President and Chief Executive Officer (2014).

Kallie graduates from FSU

Kallie, Shane, Ryan, and Jackson Rignanese

Harvey & Carol
MASSEY
FOUNDATION

- The American Diabetes Association names Harvey Massey its Father of the Year.
- Tony Massey is named Chairman of the Heart of Florida United Way Board of Directors (2014).
- The Mennello Museum of American Art recognizes Harvey Massey with its Distinguished Service Award (2015).
- Adam Scheinberg is promoted to Vice President of Information Technology, Marcelline (Marci) Baugh is promoted to Vice

President of Finance and Accounting, Ed Dougherty is named Executive Vice President of Operations and Chief Operating Officer, and Lynne Frederick is promoted to Senior Vice President of Marketing (2016).

- Adam Jones, Vice President and Director of Quality Assurance, is named President of the Florida Pest Management Association and receives the *PCT* magazine Crown Leadership Award (2016).
- The Horatio Alger Association names Harvey Massey recipient of its Horatio Alger Award (2016).

Harvey Massey at the US Capitol, 2016

Massey Services – Internal Expansion, Acquisition 2013–2016

Expansion

2013
Commercial, Clearwater, FL
Commercial, Fort Worth, TX
Residential, Plano, TX
Commercial, Jacksonville, FL
GreenUP Winter Haven, Winter Haven, FL
GreenUP Palm Harbor, Palm Harbor, FL

2014
GreenUP Avalon Park, Orlando, FL
Residential, Palm Harbor, FL
GreenUP Port St. Lucie, Port St. Lucie, FL
Residential, Ft. Myers, FL
Residential, West Osceola County, FL
Residential, Boca Raton, FL
Residential, Ormond Beach, FL
Residential, Leander, TX
Residential, Dallas, GA
Residential, Sandy Springs, GA
Residential, Winder, GA

2015
Residential, Suwanee, GA
Residential, Brandon, FL
GreenUP Brandon, Brandon, FL
Residential, Greenville, SC
Residential, Columbia, SC
Residential, Charleston, SC
Residential, Canton, GA
Residential, Cumming, GA
Residential, Edmond, OK

2016

GreenUP Port Charlotte, Port Charlotte, FL
Residential, Panama City, FL
Commercial, North Atlanta, GA
Commercial, Plano, TX
Residential, Sugarland, TX
Residential, East Houston, TX
Residential, The Woodlands, TX
Residential, Ft. Worth, TX
Residential, Northeast San Antonio, TX
Residential, Austin, TX
Residential, Moore, OK
GreenUP Windermere, Windermere, FL

ACQUISITION

2014
Austin, TX
Norcross, GA

2015
Atlanta, GA
Austin, TX
Edmond, OK
Oklahoma City, OK
Greenville, SC
Columbia, SC
Charleston, SC

2016
Dallas, TX
Houston, TX
San Antonio, TX

THE EAGLE CIRCLE

CHAPTER 10

Recognition

"It's essential to shine a light on outstanding performance."

Every business would succeed if all employees—or *team members* in the case of Massey Services—were self-motivated and consistently performed above and beyond management's expectations.

"It would be nice," Harvey Massey said, "but in the real world of business, at least, things don't really operate that way."

Back in the mid-1990s, a new nonoperational member of Massey Services' leadership team accompanied several executives on a series of unannounced visits—audit sessions, they were called—to several service centers. It was a learning experience for all involved, but especially for the new person. When the executive team reconvened back at Massey's corporate training facility the next morning, the new person wondered aloud why it appeared that, at least in a couple of cases, things didn't get done at the service center because certain individuals did not perform either up to expectations or according to existing policies and procedures.

"I don't understand why these people didn't do what they knew they were supposed to do," they said.

Everyone else in the room smiled.

"If everyone did exactly what they were supposed to do," Harvey explained, "there would be no need for management. Can you imagine a football team without coaches? An army without sergeants and captains? A film without a director?"

To be sure, most team members at Massey Services learn their responsibilities and perform those duties in accordance with established company policies and procedures. Some need occasional coaching. Some require additional training. And some, unfortunately, fail to meet the requirements of the job and are reassigned, or in rare instances, either leave voluntarily or are let go.

By the same token, some perform beyond expectation. Some receive glowing reviews from customers, supervisors, and managers. Some stand head and shoulders above their peers.

Harvey Massey was one of those overachievers throughout his career with both Orkin and Terminix. He was hired by Orkin as a sales inspector. Less than a decade later, he was named the youngest vice president in the industry-leading company's history. When he was hired as senior vice president of operations by Terminix after sixteen years at Orkin, he was charged with closing the gap between number one, Orkin, and number two, Terminix. He not only closed the gap, but he also moved Terminix into the top spot in the nation's structural pest management industry. The only reason he left was to build Massey Services from a $3.9 million purchase into an industry giant.

Along the way, Harvey was rewarded not only financially and

with career advancement, but with recognition for his achievements, innovations, and for the example he set for others.

"At Orkin, there was always recognition for excellent performance in sales," he said. "They called it 'King Bee.' I was always comfortable in sales. Not everyone is."

Harvey Massey's origin story regarding sales performance goes all the way back to his earliest days at Orkin.

"Originally, when I relocated to Austin, Texas, after I was discharged from the army, I wanted to go into real estate," he said. "I was advised by a local realtor to first meet some people and to get to know the territory. To do both, I found work with Orkin."

The next part of the story is highly personal and revelatory.

"I was still relatively new at Orkin and found myself, at times, wondering what a bright young man such as myself was doing crawling under houses to inspect for termites during the hot Texas summer. Less than eight months after Carol and I got married, our first child, our daughter Angela, was born two and a half months premature. I wasn't making a lot of money, and frankly, we needed some assistance with her care."

What Harvey Massey did would resonate with most young men and women who've found themselves in a similar quandary.

"I called my father and asked him if he could loan me two hundred and fifty dollars for medical expenses and to help me and our young family get onto more solid footing. He told me he couldn't spare it. At first, frankly, I was devastated. But it also filled me with resolve. I promised Carol and I promised myself I would never allow us to have to rely on assistance like this from anyone else, ever again."

The solution, of course, was for Harvey to throw himself

into his work, to overperform against his own already sky-high standards and expectations as well as the requirements of his sales job.

"I didn't come home until I'd made at least ten calls each and every day," he said. "Any commission salesperson knows that selling is one of the only jobs where a person can literally determine his or her own success. I worked for a company providing services that everyone deep in the heart of Texas needed. I believed in our ability to deliver on those services. And I had a young wife and a brand-new, prematurely born baby girl. I put them first, I worked hard, and I learned one of the most important lessons anyone in those circumstances can learn."

The lesson, of course, was that properly motivated, an individual can rise and do amazing things.

• • •

One of Harvey's first exposures to the power of having one's work recognized by management happened when he was asked to apply the lessons he'd taught himself about sales in Austin about an hour and a half away in San Antonio. It was Harvey Massey's first step up the ladder of success at Orkin.

Recognition received in front of one's peers is an important motivational tool and sends a compelling message. Some even find it a stronger motivator than money, position, or title. All three, of course, are designed to reward excellence and to provide an example for others.

"I've never seen myself as special," Harvey said. "I worked hard because I had responsibilities—a wife and a family—and I had a desire to do well and, if possible, excel at what I was doing. I've always believed it's a good idea in business to let people know when they're doing outstanding things. Managers and executives are often quick to focus on the negatives, what people are doing wrong. It's at least equally important, if not more so, to shine a light on standout positive performance as well."

Massey Services has a broad platform centering around recognition of team members on all levels within the company. It ranges from spontaneous "attaboys" and "attagirls" for almost any kind of praiseworthy activity, work related or otherwise, to periodic presentations at service centers and at regional and divisional meetings for outstanding operational performance. Recognition at Massey Services reaches its pinnacle at the company's annual Eagle Circle Banquet and Awards Ceremony, held every February in Orlando.

"I hear literally all the time from team members who receive something unexpected—a certificate of excellence, a longevity award, even just a phone call or a handshake—from me, from Tony or Andrea, or from someone else in upper management who references something they did that came or was brought to our attention," Harvey said. "Their gratitude is palpable. You can feel it!"

Tony Massey (left) and Harvey Massey (right) present Barbara Corino, Ray Dormer, and Tom Sorval Thirty-Year Longevity Awards.

These moments of feedback are important to Harvey, Tony Massey, Ed Dougherty, Andrea Massey-Farrell, and to everyone on the Massey Services leadership team.

"Look, I understand that money and promotions mean a lot, and of course they're important," Harvey said. "But I also

Orlando General Manager Scott Rothschild presents Service Technician Earnest Thomas with his Twenty-Year Longevity Pin.

believe, and always have believed, that personal recognition, the awareness that our team members outside the corporate office are not toiling somewhere in obscurity, that people up the line are aware of both their existence and their contributions and then demonstrate publicly their personal appreciation for what they do, is one of the most important and powerful leadership actions we can provide for a team member. These things may be small, but trust me, they really matter."

• • •

Just as nominees for Academy Awards in film often honestly say that just being nominated is a huge honor, only about 25 to 30 percent of Massey's over 2,500 team members are invited, along with a guest, to the company's annual Eagle Circle Banquet and Awards Ceremony. It's held on or near the February 20th anniversary of the closing of the sale of the Walker Chemical and Exterminating Company to Harvey Massey in 1985.

"The first couple of years, annual awards were handed out in the living room of our home in Longwood," Harvey said, smiling. "When it got big enough, we moved it to a small ballroom at the Sheraton Hotel in Maitland. Our last banquet—it's a black-tie affair, by the way, featuring almost fifteen hundred guests—was held in February of 2020, just before the COVID-19 pandemic closed things down. Suffice it to say, it has turned into a very big deal for me, for my family, for the rest of the staff, and for our team."

Simply being invited to the Eagle Circle Banquet is often viewed as an honor, because on the technician, specialist, and service manager level, as well as the office administrator

Over 1,500 Massey Services team members and guests at the 2020 Eagle Circle Awards Banquet

and corporate departmental levels, it's an indication that an award or some other kind of public recognition may be in the offing. For some, it might be the only time they'll be invited to a formal black-tie event. It's sometimes the only occasion at which they'll be able to network and visit one-on-one with the entire corporate leadership team, including Harvey Massey, Tony Massey, Ed Dougherty, Andrea Massey-Farrell, Jean Nowry, and the rest of the people who lead Massey Services.

"We put a lot into the Eagle Circle Banquet," Harvey said. "It's our flagship event, and we want to make it special for everyone. It's a big deal for us as well because we get to spend some time with the people directly responsible for our company's success. Everyone on the corporate leadership team knows and under-

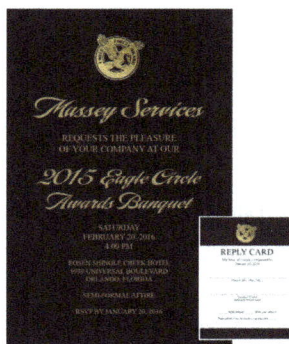

Massey Services Eagle Circle Banquet Invitation

stands that this night is for the highly valued team members who have excelled in representing Massey Services to our highly valued customers."

The multimedia event can run six or seven hours, including

dining and dancing, and features the presentation of dozens of cherished annual awards. For a few, there are actual bronze eagles, the highest award bestowed for top achievement in sales, operational leadership excellence, and corporate performance. There are president's awards and chairman's awards, given at Tony Massey's and Harvey Massey's sole discretion, which are typically beyond quantifiable measurements. There are dozens of longevity awards given to team members with a minimum of five years' service, all the way up to thirty-five years or even longer tenure with the company.

The high point for many in the room is a video collage featuring images of team members from the company's 166-plus service centers and the corporate office. It's assembled to give everyone in attendance the chance to glimpse almost everyone else in the company.

"We've gotten quite big over the past ten years or so," Harvey said. "It's difficult, if not impossible, for some of us to get to know all of the people across nine states who contribute to our company's success. Eagle Circle is something we hope every team member will aspire to attend so we can thank them in person for what they do for Massey Services."

• • •

Massey Services and its people also receive recognition from the pest management and landscape services industries, as well as the company's Central Florida headquarters community, among others. It's an important brand-connected byproduct of the company's astounding growth and success.

"Recognition of Massey Services is wonderful," Harvey Massey said, "but for the most part, it's not something we actively pursue or expect. Our priorities, as outlined in our mission statement, are to take care of our customers and our team members and to support our industry and our community."

There will be more about community involvement and investment in the next chapter of *When Your Name Is On the Door*.

For the first five or six years following Harvey Massey's purchase of the Walker Chemical and Exterminating Company in 1985, Harvey's focus was on establishing the business's foundation and stabilizing all the fundamental policies and procedures necessary to ensure controlled and consistently profitable growth.

"After we executed the purchase and changed our name to Massey Services," he said, "we did everything possible to tighten our systems and ensure we were doing the right things and, more importantly, doing those things right and doing them when they needed doing."

Moving into the status of "community leader" was another thing Harvey didn't actively pursue. He understood the value of visibility; he did, after all, appear in Massey Services' television commercials, and he did offer the pest management industry's first ever money-back guarantee in those televised commercials.

"The feedback was immediate, and it was impressive in its scope. People I didn't know called, introduced themselves, and complimented us on our advertising approach. I started meeting folks, and things happened kind of as a matter of course."

An early bit of recognition for Massey Services came via the National Pest Control Association, as it was then named in 1992. It was an award recognizing advertising merit for a newly created sales presentation folder.

"We were attempting to do something that was more

elaborate and a step up from what other companies our size were doing at that time," he said. "We didn't use models to represent either our team members or our customers. We used Massey Services team members and actual customers."

Massey Services' agency, Todd Persons Communications, drafted the verbiage used in the folder. Harvey personally reviewed and edited it. He was concerned with the accuracy of the information provided, but he also didn't want to, as he put it, "do too much selling." He wanted the folder to educate both team members and potential customers.

"We have always subscribed to the theory in all our advertising and marketing materials of under promising and overdelivering."

There would be several additional instances of company recognition for its marketing, advertising, and public relations initiatives. A comprehensive listing of individual, pest management industry, and community-based recognition appears at the conclusion of each chapter of *When Your Name Is On the Door*.

A handful of initiatives for which Harvey and the company are especially grateful flow from activities involving the environment. In 1995, the agency brought a unique proposition to Harvey. Would Massey Services consider being a sponsor of educational and informative events surrounding Central Florida's observance of Earth Day?

"We were, at first, skeptical of this request," Harvey recalled. "After all, companies in the pest prevention and termite protection business were not traditionally or typically considered friends of the environment."

Despite some concern on the part of a few operations

executives, Harvey, along with representatives from the agency, met with local organizers of Earth Day activities in Orlando, Florida.

"They weren't only asking for financial support," Harvey said. "They actually asked us to participate in some of the educational and informational presentations. We reviewed things with our technical and training people, our in-house entomologist and agronomist, our vendors, and our public relations people."

Where a few were concerned with the possibility of a potentially negative outcome, Harvey decided the risk, while there, was minimal, but the potential upside was significant.

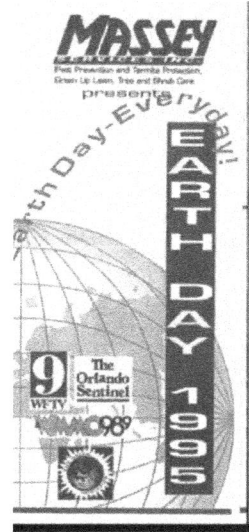

1995 Earth Day Sponsorship

"I think about this often," he said. "As it turned out, our participation was a major success and resulted in a great deal of positive publicity for our pest prevention approach, for our openness involving our products and practices, all of which further separated us from the past control practices of some unenlightened operators in our industry."

Massey Services received a community service award from the Professional Lawn Care Association of America (PLCAA) for being involved as an Earth Day sponsor. In 2001, the Orange County (Florida) Environmental Protection Division bestowed its Award of Excellence on Massey Services. This was followed by consecutive years of recognition from the US Environmental Protection Agency, in 2003 and 2004, as a "champion" of its

Pesticide Environmental Stewardship Program (PESP), which led to further recognition from state and national industry organizations and publications.

"As an operator, I never really bought into the belief that because we worked with certain types of products that our company and our industry couldn't be environmentally responsible. Our entire existence as a company, and an industry, relies on our abilities and professionalism in protecting the health, food, and property of our customers, as well as the quality of our environment."

Even when it might have been risky, Massey Services has always chosen to live its mission statement.

"Our stated purpose," Harvey said, "our reason for being, in fact, is to provide beneficial services that protect health, food, property, and the quality of our environment."

Massey Services continues to live its mission statement as is evident in the breadth and diversity of recognition that has been bestowed upon the company, on Harvey himself, and on others in the company's leadership.

Media organizations focused both on the industry and the general public consistently rank Massey Services at the top of their service delivery segments. Since Massey Services' fledgling days, government entities; industry trade groups and publications; nonprofits; educational, health-care, leisure, and recreational organizations; and both large and small arts and cultural groups have publicly praised and recognized Massey Services, its people—especially Harvey Massey and others on the leadership team—and its connection with its industry and the communities where it does business.

"All of the recognition we've received over the years wouldn't matter and likely wouldn't have happened but for the success of our company, which has simply been a byproduct of the extraordinary work of our people. I am immensely proud of each and every one of them," Harvey said.

That's how it has been, and that's how it always will be.

Moments, Milestones, Movement

Chapter 10: 2017–2019

- Ashley Rignanese graduates from Florida State University with a BS in psychology (2017).

- Harvey Massey is named CEO of the Year by the *Orlando Business Journal* and is honored with the H. Clifford Lee Lifetime Achievement Award by the Association of Fundraising Professionals (2017).

Ashley Rignanese Graduates Florida State University 2017

- In 2018, Harvey Massey is awarded the Golden Eagle from the Boy Scouts of America.

- The Harvey and Carol Massey Foundation awards $3 million to the Dr. Phillips Performing Arts Center, Orlando (2018).

- Rick Beard is named Vice President of Commercial Services (2018).

- Harvey Massey receives NPMA's Pinnacle Award, and Tony Massey receives Junior Achievement's Spirit of Achievement Award (2018).

Left to right: Harvey and Carol Massey, Tony and Jann Massey, James and Andrea Massey-Farrell

- Jonathan Goetz is named Regional Vice President (2019).

- The Massey Services 401(k) plan is awarded three National Signature Awards (2019) by the Plan Sponsor Council of America, including Best in Show.

- Sean Massey graduates from the University of Alabama (2019).

Sean Massey with his fiancée, Anna Martin

Massey Services – Internal Expansion, Acquisition 2017–2019

Expansion

2017

Residential, Raleigh, NC
Residential, Charlotte, NC
GreenUP, Alpharetta, GA

2019

Residential, Gainesville, GA
Residential, Fuquay-Varina, NC
Residential, Decatur, GA
GreenUP Orange Park, Orange Park, FL

Acquisition

2017

Residential, Charleston, SC
Residential, Charlotte, NC
Residential, Raleigh, NC

2018

Residential, San Antonio, TX
Residential, Rumble, TX

2019

Charlotte, NC
Raleigh, NC
Plano, TX

Harvey and Carol Massey at the Central Florida Veterans Memorial Park.

CHAPTER 11

Outreach and Philanthropy

"You make a living by what you get. You make a life by what you give."

The French refer to it as *noblesse oblige*: the inferred responsibility of the privileged to act with generosity and nobility toward those less privileged. Call it outreach, charitable giving, donation, sponsorship, and ultimately, philanthropy.

To some in the American business community, especially publicly traded companies burdened with meeting the quarterly expectations of analysts and investors anxious for the highest possible returns, this concept is, if not dismissed entirely, then certainly minimized. That thought never occurred to Harvey Massey. He's contributed proactively to causes, organizations, activities, and entities engaged in helping others for almost his entire adult life.

"I think, in some cases, it's a kind of DNA thing," he said. "I don't really recall a time since we began Massey Services when we weren't involved in some form of charitable giving."

Harvey's ideas of giving were influenced by him learning

about the generosity of his grandfather Samuel Corte, with whom he shared an important relationship growing up. A part of that relationship included at least weekly attendance at St. John's, the small Roman Catholic church in Melville, Louisiana.

"As I recall, it was at the funeral service after he passed," Harvey said, "that I found out he had donated the property the church was built on. He also made a sizable cash donation to help with construction. I never knew that growing up. Learning about it definitely made an impression."

Decades before forming the Harvey and Carol Massey Foundation, the Masseys were and remain today significant supporters of their church. So much so, in fact, that for a time, Harvey Massey served on the board of advisors to the Pontifical Irish College, located in Rome.

"I believe faith-based organizations are where most people are introduced to making charitable donations," he said. "There's a difference, though, in supporting one's church and getting involved in community-based giving. The emotional connection people have toward their faith is much different and can be much stronger than most secular charitable giving."

Massey Services and the Massey family are involved in both proactive and responsive programs of giving. The Harvey and Carol Massey Foundation, led by the Massey's youngest daughter, Andrea Massey-Farrell, provides philanthropic support to worthy recipients in Central Florida, the company's home base, as well as throughout the marketplaces where Massey Services does business. They are also active in Montana, where Harvey and Carol own and operate a cattle ranch and where the family spends much of its out-of-the-office time.

"I never forgot Winston Churchill's words: 'You make a living by what you get. You make a life by what you give,'" he said. "As the company grew and prospered, we thought it would be appropriate for us to establish the foundation as a more formal platform for community investment," Harvey said. "We also believe passionately about supporting what we see as quality-of-life initiatives in our greater Orlando hometown, in Montana, and in many of the communities where we have a significant presence."

People in the nonprofit world often reach out to successful, highly visible businesses for everything from incremental financial support, to help with governance, for major gift giving, as well as both small- and large-scale event and activity sponsorships. As Massey Services grew and increased its visibility in the community, and as Harvey, Carol, Tony, Andrea, and many other corporate, regional, and divisional leaders became equally involved in a wide variety of community-based organizations and activities, it became necessary for the company to identify general guidelines for how it would consider both financial support and personal investment of time and energy.

"There are way more causes and organizations deserving of some level of support than there are resources available, with us or with any business, for that matter," Harvey said. "One of Andrea's charges—in addition to leading the foundation, she's our senior vice president of community relations—is, within the boundaries of our ability to participate or contribute, to identify and qualify initiatives for us to be involved with."

While everything is subject to a varying degree of modification, Massey Services supports nonprofit initiatives associated with education, health, children's issues, arts and culture, recreation and sports, and human services.

"Of course," Harvey added, "a measurable portion of where we often direct our support has to do with who asks. Invariably, and as these things typically play out for most businesses, we'll hear from people inside the company or from companies with whom we do business or others in our circles outside of Massey Services, who ask us for support of an activity or effort they feel strongly about or are themselves involved with."

It would be impossible to identify every nonprofit organization that has benefited from either Harvey's, Harvey and Carol's, the Massey family's, or the company's generosity. There are several important and long-term recipients of personal leadership involvement, financial support, or both. And it's only appropriate to mention that sometimes, there is a business imperative attached to this kind company outreach.

"For example, I don't think it's any secret that we do a significant amount of business in the hospitality industry," he said. "We support the activities of both hotel and restaurant trade groups with sponsorships of their community relations activities, active membership in the organizations, and we participate in their own outreach efforts."

Members of the Massey family and the Massey leadership team all have causes, organizations, and activities they are passionate about and support personally or are supported by Massey Services. Tony and Jann Massey are personally involved with the Central Florida chapter of Autism Speaks, and dozens of Massey Services team members typically participate in their annual Central Florida Walk, which raises money to help meet the needs of people and families impacted by autism.

Tony and Jann Massey and their four sons (front row, right of Massey Services sign) lead the Massey contingent in the annual walk for the Central Florida chapter of Autism Speaks.

For decades, Carol Massey has been personally involved with the Orlando Morning Star Catholic School, a not-for-profit accredited school for children with special needs. Massey Services sponsors and participates in Morning Star's annual luncheons, golf tournaments, and other learning and fundraising activities.

Andrea Massey-Farrell, in her dual roles as SVP of community relations for Massey Services and president of the Harvey and Carol Massey Foundation, is personally involved with many organizations, including Orlando Shakespeare Festival (Orlando Shakes), Nemours Florida, and the Rollins College Hamilton Holt School, from which she is a proud graduate and sits on their board of trustees, and several others.

In addition, members of the Massey Services leadership team are all following the Massey family's example of getting and staying involved in both charitable and industry activities. For example, Executive Vice President and Chief Operating Officer

Ed Dougherty is involved with Junior Achievement and Florida Citrus Sports. Chief Financial Officer Jean Nowry sits on the board of the Orlando Ballet and United Arts of Central Florida. Senior Vice President of Customer Service Jeff Buhler's community involvement includes stints with the Orlando Science Center and the Winter Park YMCA. Senior Vice President of Marketing Lynne Frederick has supported Kids House of Seminole County and Orlando Ballet.

For more examples and information, visit www.masseyservices.com, click on About Us, and get to know the Massey Services leadership team.

• • •

Harvey Massey also values and personally participates in many activities associated with the National Pest Management Association, as well as with other industry-related national and state organizations. He encourages others to do the same and get involved with state and local industry affiliate organizations in pest management and landscape services.

"I have always believed in the idea of a rising tide lifting all boats," Harvey said. "Strong, respected pest management and landscape services industries can only serve to benefit all of its members, including Massey Services."

Some might argue Harvey Massey has taken this notion to the extreme. In his role as founder and leader of the fifth-largest company in the pest management industry and the largest family-owned-and-operated company in the industry, Harvey has, over the years, opened his doors and shared willingly and broadly with individual operators. Some have literally brought their entire management team to visit Massey's corporate facility and several service centers to understand how Massey Services has achieved its impressive record of growth, profitability, and customer retention.

When asked if he's concerned about sharing what others might consider proprietary information, he simply shakes his head.

"There are a number of reasons why we do this, and frankly, they all work to our advantage as well as to the benefit of the people and companies with whom we share. First, we know going in that a number of those who visit us to learn how we do what we do may never be able to match our performance. For one, they don't have our people. Second, if we can help make them better operators, how does that hurt us? Our industry has enormous potential for growth and customer base expansion. It's not a zero-sum game. There's plenty to go around. Finally, at some point, we may want to discuss acquiring a business we've helped to develop."

Harvey was also one of a handful of industry leaders involved in the creation and development of the Professional Pest Management Alliance (PPMA) and has been a key investor in its success. A venture under the umbrella of the National Pest Management Association, the PPMA works to enhance the image and reputation of the pest management industry through a variety of initiatives.

"PPMA grew out of the 'rising tide' philosophy," Harvey said. "At the time of its emergence some twenty years ago, our entire industry was only serving about twenty percent of the potential residential pest and termite marketplace in America. There were still a lot of do-it-yourself products available, and there were a lot of potential customers who didn't fully understand the benefits of professionally delivered pest management services."

Through its various programs, the Professional Pest Management Alliance has helped the entire pest management industry to further penetrate both residential and commercial marketplaces, and it has helped growing companies with designs on becoming the next Massey Services do better for their customers and their bottom lines.

"I know it sounds like a broken record, but once again, it all goes back to our mission statement," Harvey said. "We believe in being a contributing member within our community and in our industry. Supporting local, community-based organizations to help improve the quality of life where we live and supporting our industry to make it stronger and encourage a higher level of professionalism and respect can only be beneficial to our own standing and for every one of our customers."

Moments and Milestones, Movement

Chapter 11: 2020–2022

- Kallie Rignanese graduates from the University of Florida with a MS in health sciences (2020).
- Ashley Rignanese graduates from the University of West Florida with an MS in applied behavioral analysis (2021).
- Tony and Jann's son Sean joins Massey Services as a manager trainee (2020).
- Tony Massey is named Father of the Year by the American Diabetes Association (2019).
- John Milton (2020), Tami Swanson, and Darlene Williams (2021) are promoted to Regional Vice President.
- Andrea Massey-Farrell is named a Woman of the Year by *Orlando* magazine (2020).
- Michael Monahan joins Moxē as President and CEO (2020).
- Bryan Massey is scheduled to graduate from the University of Alabama in May 2022.

Darlene Williams, Regional VP

Tami Swanson, Regional VP

Massey Services – Internal Expansion, Acquisitions 2020–2022

Expansion

2017
Residential, Raleigh, NC
Residential, Charlotte, NC
Residential, Alpharetta, GA

2019
Residential, Gainesville, GA
Residential, Fuquay-Varina, NC
Residential, Decatur, GA
GreenUP Orange Park, Orange Park, FL

2020
GreenUP St. Petersburg, St. Petersburg, FL

2021
Residential, Denton, TX
Residential, McKinney, TX
Residential, Frisco, TX
Residential, Doral, FL
GreenUP Destin, Destin, FL

2022
GreenUP Tallahassee, Tallahassee, FL

Acquisition

2020
Baton Rouge, LA
Elgin, SC
Pompano Beach, FL
Hilton Head, SC
Houston, TX

2021

Wilmington, NC
Virginia Beach, VA
Chattanooga, TN
Cleveland, TN
Dacula, GA
Charlotte, NC

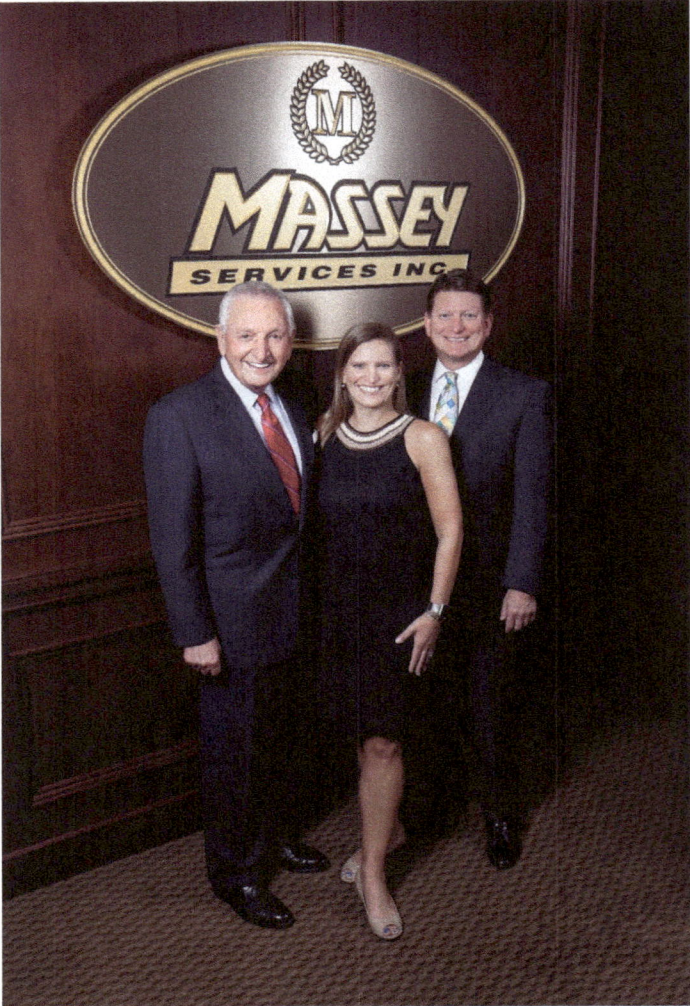

Left to right: Harvey Massey, Andrea Massey-Farrell, and Tony Massey

CHAPTER 12

What's Next?

"The future will happen. We must be prepared."

A great American philosopher, Lawrence "Yogi" Berra allegedly once said, "The future ain't what it used to be."

When asked to talk about his future or the future for Massey Services, Harvey Massey doesn't have a lot to say.

"I don't really think that much about the future in terms of grand plans," he said. "It's going to happen, and we have to do our best to be prepared. I'm eighty (as of December 28, 2021). I love what we've done and where we are as a business. Tony and Andrea are perfectly capable of moving the company forward operationally and within the communities we're privileged to serve. We tend not to tinker with our mission, vision, and values as a company."

Like his father, Tony Massey is not much for bragging, but he's fine with stating facts: "Massey Services is in outstanding financial and operational condition. We're not publicly owned, so the question really becomes whether we can continue as we have for the past thirty-six years, to grow in a sensible, controlled manner, to take care of our families, to provide opportunity for our team members, and to keep our commitments to our customers. If we can do that, the future will take care of itself."

As this book goes to its publisher, Massey Services, Inc. is doing exactly that.

Harvey's $3.9 million acquisition of the Walker Chemical and Exterminating Company, made on February 20, 1985, included its customers, employees, and vehicles, operating out of four service centers in Central Florida. Today, the Massey Services team of 2,500 members provides residential and commercial pest prevention, termite protection, landscape services, and disinfecting services to over 750,000 customers out of 166 service centers in nine states. The company that produced almost $4.3 million in its first ten months of operation should close out 2021 having generated over $318 million in revenues.

"Sometimes it's hard to comprehend that a review of our company's performance over the years since the acquisition back in 1985 reveals that we've doubled in size pretty much every five years," Tony said. "We've gone from being a small Central Florida business to a regional operation, the fifth largest in America, covering nine states. It's entirely likely we'll approach $320 million in revenue when we close out 2021."

So, what's on the horizon for Harvey Massey, for the Massey family, and for Massey Services?

"My father is still very much involved," Andrea said. "He comes to the office every day and has plenty to do. When they can and when they want to, he and our mom head for Montana and enjoy spending time at the family's ranch. Sometimes, one or

Left to right: Harvey, Angie, Carol, Andrea, and Tony Massey

more of us join them, sometimes with some of the grandkids."

Harvey and Carol Massey have been married for fifty-eight years, have three adult children, eight grandsons, and two granddaughters.

Angela and her husband, Dr. Shane Rignanese, a family physician, live in Tallahassee, Florida. They have two daughters, Kallie and Ashley, and two sons, Ryan and Jackson. Angie, like her mother, does not have a day-to-day role in the company's operation.

(Front Row) Shane and Angie (Back Row) Jackson, Ashley, Kallie, and Ryan Rignanese

Left to right: Aiden, Sean, Jann, Tony, Colin, and Bryan Massey

Tony Massey celebrated thirty-two years with Massey Services at the end of 2021. He has been president since 2006 and was appointed CEO in 2021. He and his wife, Jann (Stockman), have four boys: Sean, Colin, Bryan, and Aidan.

Andrea Massey-Farrell marks twenty-four years with the Massey organization at the end of 2021. She is currently senior vice president of community relations for Massey Services and, since 2014, has served as president of the Harvey and Carol Massey Foundation. She and her husband, James Farrell, have twin sons, Ethan and Edward (Tedy).

Left to right: Andrea Massey-Farrell, Tedy, Ethan, and James Farrell

• • •

All indications are that Massey Services' future should, for the most part, resemble it's impressive past.

"We have no reason to believe our core residential businesses won't continue to grow through both internal expansion and appropriate acquisition," Tony Massey said. "In addition, our BioAssured disinfecting service has seen a dramatic upswing due to the COVID-19 pandemic. I have confidence this segment of our commercial services business under Rick Beard will further establish itself moving forward and will continue to see higher growth levels in coming years."

Harvey, Tony, and Andrea also take an occasional glance at a map of the United States.

"We see nothing but opportunity, especially in states adjacent to those the company already serves," Tony said.

"We can't help but consider states like Mississippi, Alabama, and Arkansas for future residential and commercial expansion, most likely through acquisition," Tony said. "I'm not sure how far north and west we'd consider, but my father always taught us the wisdom in keeping options open and never saying never."

In addition to the company's established and impressive history of vertical growth, Tony Massey also considers a future open to horizontal expansion.

"Throughout the past thirty-seven years, we've made many significant changes in how we offer our core residential and commercial pest, termite, and lawn care services," he said. "We moved from pest control to pest prevention. We've taken advantage of innovations in both the products we employ and the methods we use to improve efficacy in residential termite protection. In the commercial arena, we expanded our service offering to include bedbug remediation. And in 2007, we moved into the irrigation system maintenance space."

And, in the spirit of keeping options on the table and never saying never, Tony leaves the door open to not only new markets, but new service offerings.

"If the entire COVID-19 experience has taught us anything, it's that many more people are already spending more time in their homes," he said. "They're not necessarily cloistering, but many are taking advantage of working from home and of finding more of their family entertainment options in the home. If we can find opportunities to expand our brand into other service offerings and to provide them consistent with our mission statement, why wouldn't we explore something like that?"

Tony also speaks to another question about the future of Massey Services.

"My son, Sean, who graduated from the University of Alabama in 2019, has been in our company's manager training program since the beginning of 2020 and is currently a service manager in one of our service centers," he said. "That's a bit over thirty years since I took those exact same steps. My father and mother have nine other grandchildren. If any of them have any interest in participating in our company's future, they'll have every opportunity to do so. We are the largest family-owned business in our industry, and we plan on remaining just that."

Andrea echoes her brother's sentiments. "Our father established the template for everything we do to help build community in the places where our company does business," she said. "Our mission statement is the company's North Star.

We will continue to provide community outreach, support for our industry, and do everything we possibly can to extend philanthropic efforts toward initiatives that support quality of life for our customers and for our team members."

The Massey Services Mission Statement was woven into the fabric of the company in 1991. It has remained fundamentally unaltered since then. For Harvey, Tony, Andrea, and Sean, it's embedded in the company's DNA.

"It kind of goes back to the title of this book," Andrea said. "When it's your name on the door, you operate and behave in a manner consistent with the mission, vision, and values espoused in our mission statement."

"From the way our service technicians interact with our customers," Tony added, "to the image we project in our uniforms, vehicles, and marketing materials, to our community activities and both corporate and personal philanthropy, we remain the company our father built beginning back in 1985. Whatever we do, wherever we do it, no matter how far we expand or how big we grow, those elements will never change."

Meanwhile, the men and women of Massey Services go to work every day committed to the company's mission, to its core beliefs, and to the vision put in place by Harvey Massey.

• • •

No matter who said it, it's a true statement: it's hard to predict anything, especially the future, but if, as the saying goes, past is prologue, certain things have an excellent chance of happening.

"A lot will be determined based on everyone's health," Harvey said. "We're a family of strong faith, but we all understand that some things aren't necessarily in anyone's control. So, all assumptions or considerations regarding the future—mine, our family's, or our company's—come with a simple caveat: God willing."

At the beginning of *When Your Name Is On the Door*, there was a reference to how God finds amusement in a man making plans. When he was a young man, fresh out of the Army Security Agency and heading to Texas to marry the woman with whom he would spend the rest of his life, Harvey Massey planned to sell real estate in Austin. That particular plan didn't come to fruition. Instead, his life happened. That life became a classic American personal, business, and family success story. And it's not nearly over—not by a long shot.

It couldn't have happened to a better man, a better family, or a better company.

Author's Note

My legal name is Bruce F. Katz. Due to a name change imposed when I began working in radio, on-air in Central Florida, I was known as Bud Brewer for thirty-six years, from late 1975 until I retired in 2011 and moved to Highlands, North Carolina.

I met Harvey Massey shortly before he changed the name on the door of the business he'd bought in Orlando from Walker Chemical and Exterminating Company to Massey Services. I worked closely with him and for him from then until my retirement.

Our relationship began when he retained Todd Persons Communications, where I was a vice president, to handle marketing, advertising, and public relations for Massey Services. Todd Persons, owner and president of the agency, encouraged us to bond with our clients. "Make them need you," he'd said.

I was the principal point of contact between the agency and Massey Services until 1995. At that time, and with Harvey apparently needing me, I accepted his offer to join Massey

Services as the company's first director and, in 1998, vice president of marketing.

Left to right:
Harvey Massey,
Carol Brinati,
Todd Persons

In 1997, Massey Services bought the agency, then called Persons & Brinati Communications. He changed the agency's name to Massey, Persons & Brinati, then MPB Communications, and finally to Massey Communications.

In 2003, I returned to the agency as president and CEO to help it grow and to mentor Harvey's daughter, Andrea, in the business of strategic communication, marketing, advertising, and all aspects of public and community relations. Upon my retirement, Andrea assumed leadership of the agency and remained there until formation of the Harvey and Carol Massey Foundation. Andrea Massey-Farrell was installed as president and CEO of the foundation, as well as senior vice president of community relations for Massey Services. At that point, the agency morphed once again, this time into what it is today: Moxē.

I report this in the spirit of full disclosure regarding my long, personal relationship with the Massey family and with Massey Services, and to explain how and perhaps why I was asked to author When Your Name Is On the Door.

This book is the result of a COVID-19-fueled, Zoom-enabled labor of love. Harvey and I spoke almost weekly for nearly six months as we put the narrative together. Andrea and Lynne Frederick, Massey's senior vice president of marketing, provided invaluable aid handling logistics, some gentle editing, and assembling the images that accompany the text.

I hope everyone who reads When Your Name Is On the Door will enjoy and benefit from knowing the inside story about the remarkable birth, growth, and expansion of Massey Services, the revolutionizing of an American industry, a very special man, and his equally special family.

Thank you, Harvey, Carol, Andrea, and Tony for entrusting me with this wonderful project. Thank you so very much, Lynne Frederick. This whole effort doesn't happen without your generous assistance and counsel. Thank you to all my former teammates and friends at Massey Services, and thanks to Angie and the rest of the extended Massey family. I must thank everyone who contributed personal photographs and other images to When Your Name Is On the Door. I know many may be less than perfect, but I believe the story is better with them included.

And finally, thank you, readers.

Harvey Massey and Bud (Brewer) Katz

Harvey Massey aboard Red at Checkerboard Cattle Company, the family's Montana ranch.